HOTSPOTS

TURKEY

LYC

Marmaris, Fethiye, Ölüdeniz, Hisarönü, Kalkan, Kaş, Turunç, Içmeler

Written by Lindsay Bennett
Front cover photography courtesy of Thomas Cook Tour Operations Ltd

Original design concept by Studio 183 Limited
Series design by the Bridgewater Book Company
Cover design/artwork by Lee Biggadike, Studio 183 Limited

Produced by the Bridgewater Book Company
The Old Candlemakers, West Street, Lewes, East Sussex BN7 2NZ, United Kingdom
www.bridgewaterbooks.co.uk
Project Editor: Emily Casey Bailey
Project Designer: Lisa McCormick

Published by Thomas Cook Publishing
A division of Thomas Cook Tour Operations Limited
PO Box 227, Units 15-16, Coningsby Road, Peterborough PE3 8SB, United Kingdom
email: books@thomascook.com
www.thomascookpublishing.com
+ 44 (0) 1733 416477

ISBN-13: 978-1-84157-533-9
ISBN-10: 1-84157-533-X

Head of Thomas Cook Publishing: Chris Young
Project Editor: Diane Ashmore
Production/DTP Editor: Steven Collins

Printed and bound in Spain by Graficas Cems, Navarra, Spain

CONTENTS

SYMBOLS KEY

The following is a key to the symbols used throughout this book:

information office	airport	restaurant
post office	tip	café
police station	shopping	fine dining

telephone · fax · email · website address

address · opening times · important

€ budget price €€ mid-range price €€€ most expensive

★ specialist interest ★★ see if passing ★★★ top attraction

INTRODUCTION

Getting to know the Lycian coast

IZMIR
TURGUTIU
SALIHLI
ALAŞEHIR
EŞME
ÖDEMIS
TIRE
SELÇUK
Ephesus
KUŞADASI
AYDIN
NAZILLI
Büyuk Mend. N
Pamukkale
DINAR
SÖKE
DENIZLI
ISPARTA
BURDUR
TAVAS
Salda Gölü
MILAS
MUĞLA
ULA
BODRUM
Dalaman Nehri

FETHIYE
ELMALI
Hisarönü
ÖLÜDENIZ
Saklikent Gorge
Baba Dağ
Bey Daglari
RHODES TOWN
PHASELIS
Tlos
Xanthos
LYCIAN COAST
Letoön
Patara
KALKAN
KALE
RHÓDES
KAŞ
LINDOS
MEDITERRANEAN SEA
N
BLACK SEA
SEA OF MARMARIA
TURKEY
LYCIAN COAST
MEDITERRANEAN SEA
CYPRUS
SYRIA

Getting to know the Lycian coast

What is your idea of the perfect holiday destination? Long, hot sunny days, with beautiful sandy beaches? Crystal clear seas and friendly people? Lots to see and do, but no rush to do anything? Then Turkey's Lycian coast – a touch of spice but with a few touches of home – is the place for you, whether you enjoy 'buzzing' nightlife or a quiet evening with just the buzzing of the cicadas.

A LAND RICH IN HISTORY

'Where East meets West' or 'the crossroads of history' – there are many ways to describe this land. The country stretches from the Aegean Sea in the west into the Middle East and Asia in the east, and it has been used as a land-bridge for hundreds of generations. Persians, Greeks, Romans, Byzantines and Ottomans all feature strongly in its long history and have left fascinating legacies for today's holidaymakers to explore.

VARIED NATURAL BEAUTY

If you're not a history buff, then Turkey has much more to offer. The sheer beauty of the landscape would be enough to draw the crowds, but here you can do more than simply gaze in awe. A fleet of boats cruise just offshore and jeep safaris navigate through forests, river-beds and mountain passes. Hiking trails point the way to panoramic vistas, and you can pilot a jet ski or kayak to explore the coastal shallows. If this all sounds too energetic, there is plenty of opportunity to bronze on the beach and dip your toes in the azure shallows with a beach bar just on the doorstep for that cooling drink or head to a Turkish bath for a little pampering.

EVENING ENTERTAINMENT

Nightlife is varied here: the coast's larger towns offer some of the most raucous nightlife of any holiday destination in Europe – great foam parties and fishbowl cocktails – while smaller resorts are the perfect locations for romantic meals and moonlit strolls on the beach.

Ölüdeniz – one of the most beautiful stretches of Lycian coast

FASCINATING COASTLINE

Lycia gets its name from the ancient people who called this region home during the 2nd and 1st century BC. Their legacy is a collection of spectacular rock-cut tombs and sentinel burial chambers that can be found all across the region, though the best are at Myra and Dalyan. This coastline is the most dramatic in Turkey.

In the east, sheer high peaks plunge directly into the sea. The region became a yachting and hippy paradise in the 1970s and remained off the beaten track until the early 1990s. It is not for nothing that this area is also known as the Turquoise coast; the colour of the sea really is a translucent blue-green – but there's little sand for making castles.

If it's sandy beaches you're after, you need to head to the west of the region where you'll find arguably the best beaches in the country, which you'll have the pleasure of sharing with the endangered loggerhead turtle – particularly at Patara and İztuzu. The resorts in the west, Marmaris or Hisarönü, are ideal for the fun-loving crowd – great for natural beaches and nightlife. As you travel further east the resorts become smaller but with a more upmarket exclusive feel. Both Kalkan and Kaş have great restaurants and shopping, with Kaş still being the most bohemian, laid-back spot on the whole of the Turkish coast.

The best of the Lycian coast

The Lycian coast offers a wealth of fantastic experiences that fill the hours from dawn until well after dusk.

- Marvel at the ancient **Lycian cave tombs** of Dalyan (see page 70).
- Stroll through Kayaköy's deserted streets – your only companions in this **old Greek village** will be goats and wild birds (see page 22).
- Sunbathe on the **teardrop beach at Ölüdeniz**, one of Turkey's most beautiful stretches of sand (see page 24).
- **Paraglide** from Mount Baba or Mount Asaz for great views (see page 59).
- Take a **boat trip to Kekova**, where you can gaze down through crystal clear waters to a sunken Roman town (see page 72).
- **Get covered in therapeutic mud** at the Ilıca mud baths (see page 71).
- Visit the wooden cafés perched over **Saklıkent Gorge** (see page 61).
- Take the scenic **coastal drive**. The road hugs the cliffs, through aromatic pine forests with fantastic views of remote coves.
- **Barter for a bargain** at a Turkish bazaar.

RESORTS
Places under the sun

DATÇA, ARMUTALAN HAMMAM & KNIDOS
DATÇA CADDESI
MUHARREM ELGIN BUL
BUS STATION
DALYAN
RECAT GÜREL BUL
ALIESIN SOKAK
HACI ABDI CAD
MUSTAFA MUGLALI CADDESI
HASAN ISIK CADDESI
HAMDI YÜZAK SOKAK
SEHA MERAY
Fountain Park
ULUSAL EGEMENLIK CADDESI
NURI NUR SOKAK
YENIYOL CADDESI
KONFIL ILGAZ SOKAK
UZUNYALI & IÇMELER BEACHES, ATLANTIS WATERPARK
ATATÜRK (KORDON) CADDESI
MUSTAFA KEMEL CADDESI
IRMIÇI SOKAK
CAVUSOGLU SOK
ATATURK MEYDANI
GÜZPINAR SOKAK
GÜL SOKAK
VENEDIK KANAL KENARI SOKAK
Marmaris Bay
KORDON CADDESI
TERSANE YOLU
BAZAAR
ISKELE MEYDANI
MOSQUE
HACI MUSTAFA SOK (BAR STREET)
HAMAM
EXCURSION BOATS
CASTLE
BARBAROS CADDESI
Harbour
N
0
100
200 m
Netsel Yacht Marina

Marmaris
Lycia's most energetic destination

Set in a magnificent deep bay, surrounded by rolling hills blanketed in pine forest, Marmaris has a beautiful backdrop. But it can't claim to be the prettiest town. It has developed fast in the last 15 years, and now its mainly concrete hotels and apartment blocks stretch for miles westward along Uzunyalı beach. But it certainly has the biggest choice of bars, restaurants and clubs in Lycia, and a great range of things to do and see in the surrounding countryside and coast.

HISTORY

The site was originally populated by ancient Dorians. With its naturally sheltered harbour, it seemed a good place for a settlement but was ignored through the Roman and Byzantine eras. In 1522, Suleyman the Magnificent used the bay as the embarkation point for the Ottoman army that laid siege to the Knights of St John at Rhodes. While he was waiting, he built the castle and the *han* (an Ottoman guest house), planting the seeds of Marmaris' old town.

In 1798, Nelson brought the British navy here to rest before they sailed to Egypt to defeat Napoleon's navy in the Battle of the Nile. Recent years have seen a new British invasion – this time to take over the beaches and soak up the sun.

Marmaris tourist office ⓐ Marmaris Limanı (in the port) ⓣ 0252 412 1035

THINGS TO SEE & DO

Boat trips ★★★

The day trips from the harbour are excellent and take in some beautiful off-shore islands. Cedar Island (*Şehir Adası*) is also known as Cleopatra Island because this is where the Egyptian queen enjoyed illicit moments with her lover, the Roman general Mark Anthony, who was pushing to be Caesar. It is said that Mark Anthony had the sand of the main beach imported to make it more beautiful for her. You'll be able to explore the remains of ancient Cedrae, the town where they stayed.

Other routes take you along the Bozburun Peninsula to the south-west of town. There is also a regular boat-taxi to Içmeler (pronounced Ich-meller), 9 km (5.6 miles) west along the peninsula. Here there is a good beach, plus a pretty old quarter to explore.

The castle ★★

This tiny Ottoman castle, built in the late 16th century, offers great views of the old town and the bay beyond. The castle has a museum with quite a varied collection of old Ottoman and naval artefacts, but children will probably be more interested in the wild tortoises and peacocks that roam the flower-filled courtyard gardens. Ⓐ Kaleiçi Ⓣ 0252 412 1459 Ⓛ Open 08.30–noon and 13.00–17.30 Ⓘ Admission charge

Netsel Yacht Marina ★★

The largest marina in the region, Netsel is the staging post for European flotilla groups and is also home to some of the most expensive gin palaces in the eastern Mediterranean. These are mostly owned by wealthy Turks, so shopping and dining around the marina tends to cater to their expensive needs. This is a wonderful place to stroll, especially in the early evenings.

The old town (Kaleiçi) ★★

Like a tiny pearl at the heart of Marmaris, the old town tumbles down the hill below the castle. Narrow alleyways flanked by tiny whitewashed cottages make it a relaxing place to browse with its small souvenir shops, a couple of art galleries and lots of traditional family homes.

Waterfront ★★★

Marmaris has a very attractive waterfront – *Barbaros Caddesi* – with a collection of wooden *gülets* (Turkish sailing boats) bobbing in the water and a slew of cafés and restaurants where you can enjoy an atmospheric meal or evening drink while watching the world go by.

Atlantis Waterpark ★★
This water park offers numerous water slides and rubber-ring rides with names such as Kamikaze and Black Hole, plus a bowling alley, pool bar and games throughout the day. ⓐ 212 Sokak 3, Uzunyalı ⓣ 0252 411 0462 ⓛ Open 08.30–18.00, later in summer (closing times vary seasonally)

Outdoor activities ★★
Alternatif Turizm is a well-established company for activities including river and sea kayaking, rafting on the Dalaman River, canyoning, hiking and mountain biking. ⓐ Camlik Sokak 10/1 ⓣ 0252 417 2720 ⓦ www.alternatifoutdoor.com

Spas & Turkish baths ★★
Armutalan Hamam This Turkish bath has traditional treatments, but also benefits from a sauna and Jacuzzi, combining eastern and western therapies. ⓐ Datça Caddesi ⓣ 0252 412 0710 ⓛ Open daily (check for times of mixed sessions)

BEACHES

Head west to the **Uzunyalı strip** for a beach with good water sports and rides, plus hundreds of bars and restaurants. Although it is long, it's also very narrow, so people do get packed together in summer. There are good beaches at **Içmeler** and **Turunç** that can be reached on a day trip.

SHOPPING

Marmaris has excellent shopping in every category, and its bazaar, stocked with designer fakes, spices and Turkish crafts, is one of the largest and busiest along the coast. For upmarket shopping, head to **Netsel marina** where you'll be able to find clothing boutiques, jewellers and craft shops.

Friday is market day, when families from the surrounding countryside bring their wares to sell. Pine honey is a local speciality.

EXCURSIONS

The Blue Voyage ★★★

In the 1920s, Cevat Şakir Kabaağaçlı, Turkish writer and native of Bodrum, wrote *Mavi Yolculuk* (*Blue Voyage*) about a simple *gület* journey from Bodrum in the Aegean around the Lycian coast to the south, stopping at Marmaris. It captured the imagination of a generation of Turks. **The Blue Voyage** takes several days and lets you follow in Kabaağaçlı's footsteps.

Datça and Knidos ★

The journey along the Datca peninsula west of Marmaris is spectacular, and the unsurfaced road for the final section adds to the adventure. The ancient site of Knidos sits at the peninsula's western tip and is known for its stunning sunsets. In ancient times this was a prosperous holy city, but there's little left today. The resort of Datça itself is a tiny enclave catering mainly to the yachting crowd, with a relaxed waterfront of good fish restaurants where you can enjoy a long lunch and watch the boats.

Dolmuş (minibus) services go to **Turunç** (see page 50) and **Içmeler** (see page 54), plus a bus service to **Dalyan** (see page 70), takes one hour.

RESTAURANTS (see map on page 12)

Antique Restaurant €€€ ❶ Mediterranean cuisine in a modern, refined, European-style restaurant overlooking the yachts. ⓐ Netsel Marina ⓣ 0252 413 2955 ◷ Open 11.00–16.00 and 18.00–midnight

Fellini €€ ❷ The best Italian food in Marmaris and a good location for people watching on the seafront promenade. ⓐ Barbaros Caddesi 61 ⓣ 0252 413 0826 ◷ Open 11.00–midnight

Karadeniz Sofrasi € ❸ This friendly eatery is a popular stop during your shopping trip, offering Turkish pizza, kebabs and *pide*. ⓐ Sokak 9 (in the Bazaar) ⓣ 0252 413 0733 ◷ Open 08.00–midnight

Nightlife in Marmaris is always buzzing

Pineapple €€ ❹ HIgh-quality, modern bistro-style restaurant with international dishes and an English pub upstairs. ⓐ Netsel Shopping Centre, Netsel Marina ⓣ 0252 412 0976 ⓛ Open 08.00–02.00

Planet Bollywood €€€ ❺ Excellent, authentic Indian cuisine, this new place is getting rave revues. ⓐ Barbaros Caddesi 87 ⓣ 0533 460 3707 ⓦ www.planetbollywood.tv ⓛ Open 17.00–midnight

NIGHTLIFE

Nightlife is concentrated along the Uzunyalı waterfront and in the town along Hacı Mustafa Sokak (known as Bar Street).

Bar Panorama ❻ Great views from the top of the old town. Limited space if busy. ⓐ Eski Camii Sokak ⓣ 0252 413 4835 ⓛ Open 11.00–01.00

Crazy Daisy Bar and Nightclub ❼ Dancing, foam parties and live music. ⓐ Hacı Mustafa Sokak 121 ⓣ 0252 412 4856 ⓦ www.crazydaisybar.com

Daisy Bar ❽ Show dancers, Turkish nights, cabaret, a great dance floor and foam parties. ⓐ Uzunyalı 84 ⓣ 0252 413 1754 ⓦ www.daisybar.com

Green House ❾ Probably the oldest bar in town, with loud music and a great atmosphere. ⓐ Haci Mustafa Sokak ⓣ 0252 412 5071

Fethiye
Lycia's most Turkish resort

Nestling into a rocky outcrop at the southern end of a wide bay, Fethiye is the main port of Lycia. The town has no beaches, but people are drawn here because it's a good base for lots of things to see and do. The town has a picturesque bazaar – more like a Greek agora with its shady vine canopy – offering a good range of shopping opportunities, some atmospheric outdoor dining and lots of boat and land tours.

By day, Fethiye acts as a magnet to the surrounding holiday resorts of **Ölüdeniz**, **Hisarönü** and the satellite beach area of **Çalış** (Chalush). The streets are bustling, but it's a very Turkish town, so the atmosphere is more laid back than some of the other large holiday spots on the Turkish coast. As evening falls, it is relatively quiet – for nightlife, head back to the resorts.

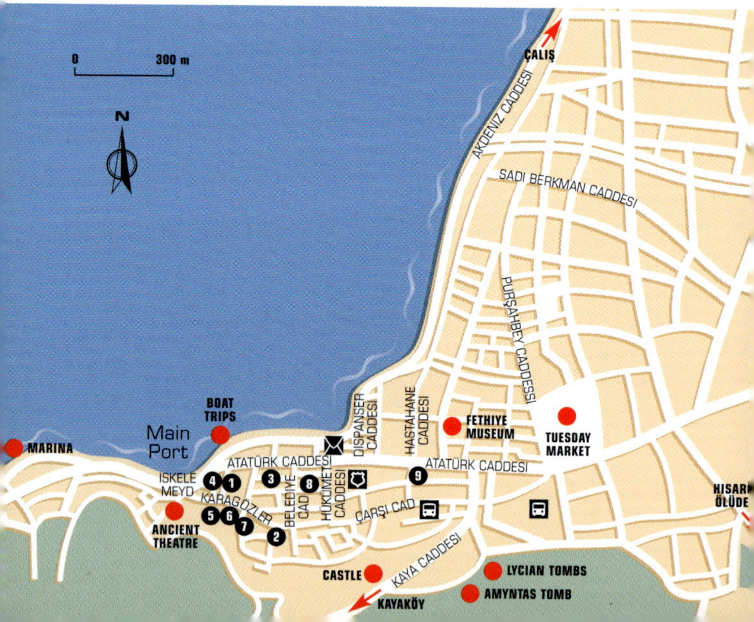

Fethiye tourist office ⓐ Iskele Meydani (by the marina)
ⓣ 0252 612 1975/614 1527

HISTORY

Fethiye was originally ancient Telmessos, founded in about 400 BC. The site has been occupied continuously since then – due to fishing and its busy port. The town was called Makri until its predominantly Greek Orthodox population emigrated to Greece in the 1920s, when it was renamed Fethiye in honour of a local war hero. Sadly, few old buildings remain because of a devastating earthquake in 1957.

THINGS TO SEE & DO

Ancient theatre ★

A tiny venue by the harbour, this Hellenistic structure was updated by the Romans. It was excavated in the 1940s. ⓐ Liman Caddesi
ⓑ 24 hours ⓘ Admission free

Amyntas tomb ★★★

Amyntas tomb is one of the largest and most beautiful along the Turquoise coast. Photographs of it feature in most tourist brochures. Carved into a sheer rock face above the town around 350 BC, it has an impressive yet simple facade of finely carved Ionic columns, rather like a Greek temple. The inside is empty. ⓐ Off Kaya Caddesi ⓣ Open 08.30–sunset ⓘ Admission charge

Boat trips ★★★

The **12-Island Boat Trip** is a must. These pine-clad islands, scattered like emeralds out across the blue velvet waters of the Gulf of Fethiye, offer some of the prettiest vistas in southern Turkey. St Nicholas Island – where the saint came to worship, and lived for many years – is a popular stop (see Myra, page 78), with its remains of an early Byzantine basilica and other 4th-century AD buildings. Most boats also stop at Şövalye for its restaurant, at Gemile for its ancient ruins and at Göcek. You can also find trips along the coast to places such as Kalkan or Patara.

Lycian tombs near Fethiye

The castle ★
Built by the Knights of St John, this small Crusader fortress – only one sturdy tower remains – was built on top of part of ancient Telmessos. It now stands above the modern town and there are good views across the bay.

Fethiye museum ★
The museum has a small collection of carved stone and statuary from sites around the region. The most important item is a *stele* (inscribed stone panel) from Letoön (see page 75) with words in three languages. This allowed archaeologists to decipher the Lycian language by translating the ancient Greek section next to it. There's also an ethnographic gallery with Ottoman artefacts. ⓐ Sokak 505, Atatürk Caddesi Ⓛ Open Tue–Sun 08.30–17.00, closed Mon ⓘ Admission charge

Lycian tombs ★★
The most obvious remains are a series of Lycian tombs carved into the crag above the town.

Diving ★
Most scuba-diving companies have bases at Çalış or Ölüdeniz, but the **European Dive Centre** is based in Fethiye town itself. ⓐ Atatürk Caddesi 8 ⓣ 0252 612 3281

Spas & Turkish baths ★★

Ece Saray Marina and Resort A full spa with facilities featuring hydrotherapy, inhalation therapies, massage, detox and other body wraps, stone therapy, reflexology and beauty facials. ⓐ Ece Sarayi, Karagözler Mevkii ⓣ 0252 612 5005 ⓦ www.ecesaray.net

Turkish bath Enjoy a cleansing massage and steam session here. ⓐ Hamam Sokak 2 ⓣ 0252 614 9318 ⓛ Check for times of mixed sessions

BEACHES

Almost a resort in its own right, **Çalış** is the major beach area for Fethiye and is only a short 5 km (3 mile) dolmuş or water-taxi ride north of the town. The two areas work well together, with Çalış having a 2 km (1.2 mile) long gravel-sand beach. Most of Fethiye's hotels lie along this strip, and there is a good range of holiday fun, from water sports to hotels, restaurants, bars and budget souvenir shops.

If you tire of the beach and town life, head to the freshwater marshes just inland. They are great for birdwatching and a haven for reptiles, amphibians and other wildlife – though they are also a good breeding ground for mosquitoes, so it would be wise to stock up on insect repellent before you go!

The pretty beach at the small resort town of **Ölüdeniz** (see page 24) is a little further away in the opposite direction.

SHOPPING

Fethiye has some good shopping, and the main souvenir bazaar around the **Hamam Sokak** in the heart of town is a wonderful mixture of cheap market stalls and top-quality, fully air-conditioned fur and leather shops, where you can buy a jacket off the peg or have one made in a few days.

A daily market at **Çarfli Caddesi** sells fake designer gear and food items, and a lively market is held on Tuesdays along the canal flanking **Atatürk Caddesi**, where local farmers bring their goods.

EXCURSIONS

Kayaköy ★★

Kayaköy was a thriving Greek village called Levissi until the founding of the Turkish Republic in the 1920s. When the Greek and Turkish governments decided to transfer their minority populations (Greeks born in Turkey were to move to Greece, and Turks born in Greece were to move to Turkey), the people of the village moved *en masse*, and Levissi became a ghost village, the largest of its kind in Turkey.

A handful of houses have been bought and restored by Europeans, and a selection of cafés (for lunch, see **Les Jardins de Levissi**, below) and tourist shops have sprung up along the roadside at the base of the town, but much of the village is now protected. Climb higher along the cobbled alleyways and you can still leave the modern world behind. Over 2000 homes still stand empty and the village – founded in medieval times – is a fascinating place to explore. The Church of Panagia Pyrgiotissa still has its frescoes and kohla'ki patterned pebble floors.

RESTAURANTS (see map on page 18)

Les Jardins de Levissi €€ ❶ A French/Turkish couple bought this mansion in the village several years ago and they provide delicious gourmet food served in a relaxing garden or dining room. ⓐ Küyübaşı mevkii Kayaköyu ⓣ 0252 618 0188 ◷ Open noon–14.30 and 19.00–22.00 ❗ Booking advised

Meğri €€€ ❷ In the heart of the bazaar, this established restaurant has a good reputation with locals. The fish is delicious, as are grilled meats, kebabs and other Turkish dishes. It also has a cheaper, less formal eatery at Çarşi Caddesi. ⓐ Lika Sokak 8–9 ⓣ 0252 614 4045/6 ◷ Open 11.00–midnight

Paşa Kebap Salonu € ❸ You'll find yourself queuing with workers from the surrounding shops and offices at lunchtime for inexpensive Turkish snacks. It's the perfect pit-stop while sightseeing or shopping. ⓐ Çarşi Caddesi ⓣ 0252 614 9807 ◷ Open 08.00–midnight

Sedir € ❹ Another longstanding favourite with the locals, serving excellent Turkish staples such as *meze* and *guveç*, plus some mouth-watering traditional puddings. It is still one of the best value places in town. ⓐ Tütün Sokak 3 ⓣ 0252 614 1095 ⓛ Open 11.00–midnight

NIGHTLIFE

The bulk of the nightlife in Fethiye sits around the bazaar, but it is more low key than the surrounding resorts, with plenty of Turkish-style cafés and bars.

Banana Bar ❺ This is a great disco-bar concentrating on the latest Euro-chart dance music. ⓐ Karagözler Sokak ⓣ 0252 612 8441 ⓛ Open 11.00–03.00

Car Cemetery Bar ❻ Great favourite for many years, this bar (with its 'car' theme – various bits of old cars form seats, counters and booths) always attracts the crowds. If you don't want a cocktail, try one of their coffees made with beans from around the world. ⓐ Hamam Sokak ⓣ 0252 612 7872 ⓛ Open 11.00–03.00

Ottoman Bar ❼ An interesting but successful mixture of Turkish pub and international disco bar, where you can spend time on the dance floor or relax on the low carpet-covered couches with a *narghile* (hubble-bubble pipe). ⓐ Karagözler Sokak ⓣ 0252 612 1148 ⓛ Open 11.00–03.00

Türkü Dostlari ❽ A more authentic evening is in store at this bar with traditional decor and Turkish music played live on traditional instruments. Live music from 23.00 nightly. ⓐ In the bazaar ⓣ 0252 614 8400 ⓛ Open 17.00–02.00

Yes Bar ❾ A good place for an early evening drink or late-night dancing. ⓐ Cumhuriyet Caddesi 9 ⓣ 0252 614 4239 ⓛ Open 11.00–03.00

Ölüdeniz
tranquil lagoon perfect for water sports

One of the most photographed beaches in the world, Ölüdeniz is a golden, teardrop-shaped stretch of shingle protecting a tranquil lagoon surrounded by fragrant pine-clad peaks. The name Ölüdeniz means 'dead sea' in Turkish and is derived from the dark motionless waters of the lagoon that have no waves at all. The landscape and coastline are definitely spectacular, with shallow, azure waters tempting you in – but there is more on offer than just the views.

In many ways, Ölüdeniz is the perfect holiday resort, with something for everyone. It's not too big, yet has a good selection of restaurants, bars and shops to enjoy. It has a beach with waves and just about every activity on the menu for water sports lovers, plus the lagoon's calm water is perfect for children and novice swimmers to splash about, and enjoy a number of non-motorized water sports.

Ölüdeniz is close to a host of places to see and things to do. Nearby **Fethiye** (see page 18) is an atmospheric town with a genuine Turkish atmosphere, while **Hisarönü**, only a couple of minutes away by regular dolmuş, is great for partying the night away.

HISTORY

Just 30 years ago, Ölüdeniz was a secret hideaway with ultra-clear waters, hidden from the rest of the world by the surrounding mountains. It started life as a hippy and backpacker haunt, with a few beach huts and tree houses to stay in, but as the 1980s progressed and the road from Fethiye was completed, more and more modern hotels were built in the valley behind the beach and the town developed into a busy resort.

Nowadays the hippies have disappeared and Ölüdeniz is a protected area, but the modern development means you get the best of both worlds – a small but lively resort combined with the magical landscapes that make this part of Turkey unique.

THINGS TO SEE & DO

Boat trips ★★

Daily trips around the bay take in Gemile beach for swimming and the Blue Cave, with a stop at Butterfly Valley (see page 27).

Kidrak Orman Parkı ★★

This natural area, just east of Ölüdeniz, marks the end of the resort and offers some shady places for a picnic or relaxing afternoon away from the hubbub.

Ölüdeniz Tabiat Parkı ★★★

The small national park, which protects the teardrop section of the Ölüdeniz lagoon from development, has a couple of basic cafés and some sports rental stands for kayaks and pedalos, plus shady areas for picnicking. You don't need to pay an entry fee if you enter the park along the beach.

Diving ★

DiveMed Diving Centre This company runs competent training and guided diving programmes. ⓐ Belcekiz Beach ⓣ 0252 617 0450 ⓦ www.meddiving.com

Spas & Turkish baths ★

Belcekiz Beach Resort Discover the *hamam* experience at this slightly touristed Turkish bath ⓐ At the hotel on the seafront. ⓣ 0252 617 0077 ⓦ www.belcekiz.com

Seawater therapy and total wellness/fitness centre This state-of-the-art thalassotherapy centre offers various body treatments from lymph drainage and algae body wraps to reflexology, massage, facials and body peels, plus a sauna and Turkish bath. ⓐ Lykia World Resort, PK 102 Ölüdeniz ⓣ 0252 617 0200 ⓦ www.lykiaworld.com

Tohum Meditation Centre For a truly holistic experience, visitors can come here for a week or two of peace and quiet away from the world, with organic meals and daily meditation and massage treatments. Alternatively, you can book by the session. The centre offers classes such as yoga and tai chi for beginners. ⓐ White Cape, Ölüdeniz, in the hills above Butterfly Valley ⓣ 0252 330 5262 ⓦ www.tohum.com

BEACHES

The pebbly **Belcekiz beach**, just east of the Ölüdeniz lagoon and in front of the hotel strip, offers an unrivalled selection of water sports – waterskiing, windsurfing, parasailing and inflatable banana boats.

SHOPPING

The Ölüdeniz resort has a range of shopping along the tangle of streets behind the waterfront, but most of what's on offer is mass-produced run-of-the-mill stuff. For better shopping, head to Fethiye (see page 18).

It is also the landing point for the paragliders, so they 'drop in' regularly throughout the day. Along the waterfront is a good range of cafés and bars for refreshment and sustenance.

The western tip and the lagoon itself concentrate on more sedate pursuits – snorkelling, kayaks and pedalos – to protect the delicate environment of the lagoon. You can rent these from the concession within the national park. This is also the best spot for quiet sunbathing, away from noisy jet skis and motor boats. The finest sandy beaches are around the inner lagoon, though none of them are very big. Most have been taken over by bars or *pensiyons* who may charge you a fee to enter.

EXCURSIONS

Butterfly Valley ★★

The floor of this 350 m (1150 ft) deep canyon, which lies at the base of **Baba Dağı**, is the perfect environment for butterflies and moths. There are over 70 species that can be seen here, including the rare Tiger Butterfly (*Euplagia quadripunctaria*), in a verdant natural landscape. The 10 hectare park is a delightful place to explore, with a magnificent 60 m (200 ft) waterfall at its landward limit into the gorge. This area has been cultivated for many centuries and is still full of fresh fruit and vegetables.

There is a minibus transfer from Ölüdeniz to the park throughout the day or a boat trip once a day. ⓐ 10 km (6 miles) east of Ölüdeniz – can only reached by boat ⓣ 0533 212 2362 ❶ Admission charge

The beautiful teardrop-shaped beach at Ölüdeniz

Kayaköy ★★

There is a wonderful walk to Kayaköy (see page 22) on the marked path that leads up into the hills from behind the Ölüdeniz lagoon. Take water for the journey, but you'll find cafés once you get to Kayaköy.

Fethiye ★★

The nearby town of Fethiye (see page 18) offers authentic Turkish flavour.

RESTAURANTS (see map on page 24)

Buzz Bar & Grill € ❶ This place, which is also an Internet café, has been open forever and everyone comes here for drinks, snacks and meals throughout the day. The food is good and evenings are really lively, helped by perhaps the best cocktails in town. ⓐ Deniz Plaji ⓣ 0252 617 0450 ⓛ Open 08.00–02.00

Sultan Peper €€ ❷ Good tourist eatery with the usual range of Turkish meals, plus a long menu of continental dishes, like pizzas, and a nightly Indian buffet for curry, bahgee and samosa fanatics. If everyone in the family fancies something different, this is the place to be. ⓐ 2 Sokak ⓛ Open 08.00–01.00

White Dolphin (Yenaz Yunus) €€€ ❸ A highly regarded restaurant – one of the best along the whole Turkish coast – serving excellent seafood and European cuisine. Enjoy wonderful views of the coast and magnificent sunsets from the terrace. ⓐ Belcekiz Beach ⓣ 0252 617 0068 ⓛ Open noon–14.30 and 18.00–midnight ⓘ Booking recommended

---

Remember, it is really easy, and worth the trip, to take a dolmuş up the hill to Hisarönü (see page 30) for more restaurants and nightlife.

NIGHTLIFE

Help Beach Bar ❹ This is a lively bar and one that has been open for a number of seasons. Great (loud) music and always a buzzing atmosphere. ⓐ Hamkamp Sokak (by the beach) ⓣ 0252 617 0498 ⓛ Open 08.00–03.00

Tequila Cocktail Bar ❺ The music at Tequila ranges from the 1960s and 1970s through to classic rock, jazz and blues, so there should be something to please everyone. As the name suggests, they serve a mean cocktail. ⓐ 1 Sokak ⓛ Open 11.00–03.00

Hisarönü
great nightlife with an English slant

It seems odd that one of Turkey's most successful resorts isn't by the sea. But when you get here, you realize why it is so popular – the place is buzzing after dark, with some of the best entertainment and nightlife along the coast, and during the day there is a great choice of things to see and do within easy reach.

Lively Hisarönü sits high in the hills above Ölüdeniz and Fethiye

Every day the town empties as people head the couple of kilometres south to the great beaches at **Ölüdeniz** (see page 24), with their fantastic range of water sports. Alternatively, many visitors take the 15-minute dolmuş ride into Fethiye for great Turkish atmosphere and fantastic shopping.

There's a raft of excursions and some exhilarating sports right on the doorstep (from microlighting to swimming with dolphins, see pages 58–60), offering all the ingredients for a young, fun holiday in the sun.

Hisarönü sits in the hills high above Ölüdeniz and Fethiye, so it is often cooler than the coastal resorts. In summer, people say it is much easier to sleep here because the air is fresher, but early or late in the season (April–May and October) you may need a sweater if you wish to dine outside under the stars.

HISTORY

When the government became concerned about tourist development at Ölüdeniz, builders looked for another location, and Hisarönü, just up the hill, hit the jackpot. Most of the resort is newly built, but you'll still find one or two reminders of the farming village that used to be here before package tourism arrived.

THINGS TO SEE & DO

When you stay at Hisarönü you can enjoy all the activities and sites of **Ölüdeniz** (see page 24) and **Fethiye** (see page 18), and there are regular, local dolmuş services to both places.

SHOPPING

There is a lively market every Monday, plus shops along the main street. For a better range of shops, catch the local dolmuş to Fethiye.

RESTAURANTS

Domino's €€ This restaurant has been open for well over a decade and still serves good international food. The menu includes English, Italian and, of course, Turkish dishes, so you should find something to suit you. There's a lovely fire in the dining room for chilly spring or autumn evenings. ⓐ Cumhuriyet Caddesi ⓣ 0252 616 6985 ◷ Open 11.00–01.00

Dragonaro €€€ The best Chinese restaurant in town – great if you fancy a change from Turkish or English food. It is always on the list of the best restaurants, and serves a full range of authentic dishes, including a vegetarian section on the menu. You'll need to book because it's usually crowded. ⓐ Just off the Kayaköy Road ⓣ 0252 616 7757 ◷ Open 08.00–midnight

The Olive Tree Restaurant and Bar €€ One of the prettiest and most relaxing places to eat in the resort, the Olive Tree offers some really good Turkish food and a range of European dishes with vegetarian options. The restaurant has built up a good reputation since it opened in the mid 1990s. ⓐ Cumhuriyet Caddesi ⓣ 0252 616 6361 ◷ Open 08.30–16.00 and 18.00–midnight

Robin Hood Restaurant & Bar €€ Not a very Turkish name, but Robin Hood serves arguably the best Turkish food in Hisarönü, plus the usual British staples and continental dishes. ⓐ By the dolmuş station ⓣ 0252 616 7859 ◷ Open 08.00–midnight

NIGHTLIFE

The Fez Café and Cocktail Bar A popular Hisarönü meeting place, the Fez has a good beer garden and serves English pub grub. There is even a weekly pub quiz every Thursday. The bar also has widescreen TVs for those unmissable Premiership matches. ⓐ Off Cumhuriyet Caddesi on the Kayaköy Road ⓣ 0252 616 6297 ◷ Open 11.00–05.00

Just 15 minutes from Hisarönü, Fethiye offers the finest shopping in the area

Zombie Bar This is a great cocktail and dance bar with a wide range of music, from hip hop to R&B. There are also widescreen TVs showing football and TV favourites. It's always lively in the evenings. ⓐ Cumhuriyet Caddesi 40 ⓣ 0252 616 6080 ⓑ Open 11.00–05.00

Kalkan
Lycia's prettiest marina resort

Cascading down a steep hillside to its pretty port and yachting marina, Kalkan is one of the most anticipated anchorages of the famed 'Blue Cruise'. This upmarket pit stop also offers high-class dining and shopping for the jet-set sailors who step ashore throughout the summer.

The cobbled lanes at the heart of town, with their converted, late-19th-century mansions, offer an atmospheric place for a evening stroll or perhaps a bit of bargaining over that must-have souvenir.

Kalkan came late to package tourism, but it has been catching up fast, particularly amongst those who want something a little more genteel than the high-energy destinations such as **Hisarönü** (see page 30) or **Marmaris** (see page 12). In the last ten years the resort has expanded rapidly out across the surrounding hillsides, but it hasn't overwhelmed the laid-back ambiance of the old village or the jaunty nautical atmosphere of the harbour side.

HISTORY

Kalkan doesn't have a very long history. The name means 'quay' or 'jetty' in Turkish, and traders from Kastellorizo (see page 46) established a marketplace here (the only decent harbour between Fethiye and Kaş) approximately 200 years ago.

By the late 19th century, Kalkan was an important port for the goods brought from the Patara and Elmelı plains (see pages 46 and 83). The fresh produce, olive oil and grain loaded here made its way to Ottoman ports all around the eastern Mediterranean.

The town continued to thrive in the early years of the Turkish Republic but began to lose importance in the 1950s as transport links were modernized. The first Lycian coastal road was completed in the early 1960s, so the port was no longer needed and most of the population moved away. At around the same time, the first tourists arrived – intrepid, wealthy foreigners sailing their yachts into the

Kalkan boasts Lycia's prettiest harbour on an atmospheric seaside town

harbour, while bohemian Turks (including one of Turkey's first rock stars) began to renovate the old houses as *pensiyons*, which introduced the Turkish upper classes to the resort.

Once the road from Kalkan to Fethiye was sealed in 1984 and Dalaman airport opened, the resort began to open up to package tours.

The Blue Cave – the largest in Turkey

THINGS TO SEE & DO

Water sports ★

Blue Marlin water sports A range of activities including sailing, jet skiing, windsurfing and fishing from the harbour area. ⓐ Hotel Pirat, Kalkan Harbour ⓣ 0242 844 2849

Canoeing ★★

Enjoy a day kayaking around Patara National Park and the Xanthos River with qualified and insured guides. **Abi Travel** also arrange other excursions to surrounding attractions. ⓐ Yali Bolu Mah 8 ⓣ 0242 844 2694 ⓦ www.abitravel.net

Diving ★★

Take training towards dive qualifications or simply do an accompanied dive to discover the sport. There are a couple of wrecks just off shore, including the 19th-century *Duchess of York*, built in Hull. **Dolphin Scuba Team** (t 0242 844 2242) and **Barracuda Dive Centre** (t 0242 844 3955 w www.dive-turkey.com) are both in Kalkan harbour and have qualified instructors and dive guides.

BEACHES

Kalkan is not renowned for its beaches. Most swimming takes place in concrete lidos or directly from the rocks. **Ibo** is a small sandy beach to the left of the harbour, and there's another shingle stretch a few minutes walk south of the resort centre. The best by far is at **Kaputaş**, 7 km (4 miles) east at the mouth of the gorge (see below). Kaputaş beach has a spectacular setting but there are no water sports and few amenities, so you will need to take provisions.

EXCURSIONS

Bezirgan ★★

This large farming community set on a verdant plain used to be the summer grazing and farming lands of the inhabitants of Kalkan, and much of the population would live here. It is still a vibrant place and provides an interesting contrast to the chic lifestyle of the coastal resort. a About 17 km (10.5 miles) inland from Kalkan

Owlsland ★★

Erol and Pauline, a Turkish/Scottish couple, have renovated Erol's traditional family farm and now offer accommodation, meals and full-day guided walking tours of Bezirgan, taking in the unexcavated ancient site of Pirha and Lycian rural lifestyle. a Bezirgan t 0242 837 5214 w www.owlsland.com Tours daily in summer ! Admission charge; eight people max, with collection from Kalkan and lunch included

Kaputaş Gorge ★★★

Cuts from the coastline deep into the Lycian foothills. Several companies run canyoning routes down the river for a high-action morning or afternoon (see Kaş for details, page 42). a 7 km (4 miles) east of Kalkan

SHOPPING

Kalkan has very good shops selling fashions, jewellery, antiques and carpets. A lot of wealthy Turks have summer houses in Kalkan, or spend the summer in rented villas, so there are also a few design studios selling modern Turkish and international furniture and house furnishings. Prices are higher than at other towns along the coast, but quality is also high.

If your budget doesn't run to this kind of thing, there are still a few more run-of-the-mill souvenir shops in the old town.

Boat trips ★★★

Kalkan has a great range of boat trips, and you could probably spend two or three days exploring the different routes on offer. The trips also get you to locations, including several cave systems, that you can't reach by car or dolmuş.

The two caves of Güvercinlik and Güvercini Güvercinlik lies at the mouth of one of the few freshwater streams that cut through the Lycian Mountains, making the water cooler than in other caves. It is also home to a population of wild pigeons and is an important bat roost. Güvercini cave is 40 m (44 yds) long and 30 m (100 ft) high, but is too narrow at the entrance for a tour boat to go inside. ⓐ 5 km (3 miles) along the coast.

The Blue Cave This is the largest sea cave in Turkey, famed for the deep blue colour of the water (best seen from inside the cave looking out). The cave used to be a habitat for rare Mediterranean seals, but they have disappeared since the boat trips started.

Other tours Alternative boat tours often head out around the small **Rat and Snake Islets** just off-shore. You could stop at **Pinar Kürü**, a pine-shaded rocky bay with very clear water that's ideal for snorkelling, or visit

Take a dip in the crystal-clear waters

Kaputaş beach – the best in the area – where you can also explore **Kaputaş Gorge** (see page 37) just inland, or **Gerenlik Bay**, which has a reasonable sandy beach and is usually deserted because there's no access for vehicles.

Other favoured anchorages are **Firnaz Bay**, a natural harbour 20 minutes out of Kalkan, or **French Bay** (east of Kalkan Bay), a popular stop for a swim.

There are local dolmuş services that go to Saklıkent Gorge (see page 61). They also frequently run to Gelamiş/Patara (see page 83), Fethiye (see page 18), Kale/Demre (see page 78) and Kaş (see page 42)

RESTAURANTS

Doy Doy €€ You will find excellent *meze* and Turkish salads in this restaurant, plus a good choice of fresh seafood, all with views over the port. ⓐ Yalıboyu Mah ⓣ 0242 844 3114 ⓛ Open 11.00–midnight

A number of Kalkan's restaurants serve traditional Turkish cuisine

Kaptan Restaurant €€ Enjoy local dishes and fresh seafood at this small, family-owned restaurant. Ⓐ Yalıboyu Mah Ⓣ 0242 844 3166 Ⓛ Open 11.00–midnight

Korsan €€€ This is about the oldest restaurant in town, having drawn the crowds since the late 1970s. It is the perfect place to start your exploration of Turkish cuisine, with good quality dishes served in a smarter setting than the usual *lokanta* without being overpriced for its beachside setting. Ⓐ Yalıboyu Mah Ⓣ 0242 844 3622 Ⓛ Open 11.00–midnight

Merkez Café € This is a great place to come and fill up on inexpensive Turkish snacks, such as *pide*, pizzas and kebabs. It's right in the heart of town, so is ideal for a lunch stop or to ward off the post-beach hunger pangs. Ⓐ Nolu Sokak 2 Ⓛ Open 08.00–midnight

Ottoman House €€€ Good Turkish cuisine is served in a lovely setting and the roof is decorated in the old Ottoman style. After your meal, you can enjoy a *narghile* (hubble-bubble pipe) with your Turkish coffee. Ⓐ Yalıboyu Mah 35 Ⓣ 0242 844 1013 Ⓛ Open 18.00–midnight

Paprika Restaurant €€ Some of the best pasta dishes in the region are found at this courtyard restaurant, along with a range of local dishes. Ⓐ Yalıboyu 12/Nolu Sokak 1 Ⓣ 0242 844 1136 Ⓛ Open 18.00–midnight Ⓘ Booking is advised because it's very popular

NIGHTLIFE

Kalkan isn't known for its loud nightlife. Most after-dinner entertainment involves enjoying a drink and conversation at a waterside café or bar.

Yacht Point This is the must-visit late-night music spot on the waterfront. Earlier in the evening, it's a great place to sit with a drink and people watch. Ⓐ Yalıboyu Mah Ⓛ Open 11.00–03.00

Kaş
bohemian and laid back

Kaş (pronounced Kash) has the most dramatic setting of any Lycian resort, lying in the shadow of jagged Ak Dag mountain, it's name means 'eyebrow' or 'something curved' and is taken from the shape of its setting at the head of a curved natural inlet.

Clinging to its rocky coastline like a limpet, this tiny settlement of narrow cobbled streets and whitewashed Ottoman houses drips with pink bougainvillea and is surrounded by azure waters to the south and pristine pine-forested peaks to the north.

The first foreign tourists to discover Kaş were hippies and sailors, and the town still has the most relaxed and offbeat feel of any Turkish resort. This is for low-energy holidays – for high energy, head to **Hisarönü** or **Marmaris**! Kaş keeps its character because, even today, it is a sailor's paradise and the most difficult Lycian resort to reach by road. It has the longest transfer from both Antalya and Dalaman airports to the east and west, so it rarely gets swamped by vast numbers of tourists.

HISTORY

Kaş was ancient Antiphellos, an important Lycian trading town and port. Later it became a quiet backwater, a mostly rural community where families fished in the winter and, during the summer months, raised sheep and grew crops on the plateau behind the Lycian mountains.

In the late 18th century, Kaş and Kastellorizo (the tiny island just off shore) were an important centre for shipbuilding, mainly controlled by the Greek section of the population. During this time, many of the fine mansions of the town were built. After the exchange of Greek and Turkish populations in the 1920s, Kaş settled back into anonymity.

During the 1930s, Kaş was rediscovered by Turkish intellectuals, but there was not a decent road around the Lycian coast until well into the 20th century, so it remained a remote region – everything had to come in and go out by boat. In the 1960s, word got out about this fantastic

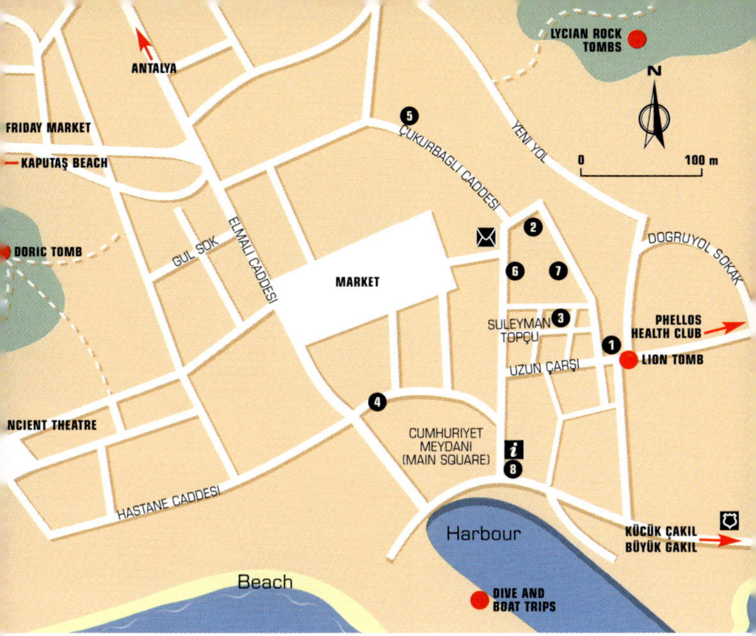

hidden gem, and Kaş became one of the most popular locations on the 'hippy trail'.

THINGS TO SEE & DO

Boat trips ★★

Boat trips are the best way to appreciate the wild beauty of the coast around Kaş, leading to many remote coves that are inaccessible by car, including the largest sea cave in Turkey, the **Blue Cave** (see page 38). There are regular trips to the long, turtle-nesting beach at **Patara**, where you can spend the day sunbathing or exploring the ancient remains just inland amongst the dunes (see page 83). Other popular destinations include the easily accessible, off-shore islets of **Liman Ağzi** and **Longos**.

Kaş tourist office ⓐ Cumhuriyet Meydani 5
ⓣ 0242 836 1238

Ancient theatre ★

The ancient theatre in Kaş is small by the standards of others in Turkey, but has been renovated.

Doric Tomb ★

Cut into the hillside that forms the back of the theatre, this tomb was carved in the 3rd century BC.

Lion Tomb ★★

One of the largest Lycian tombs in the region, Lion Tomb sits squarely at an intersection in the middle of town and is usually draped with carpets for sale at the surrounding shops. It gets its name from the handles of the tomb lid, which are carved into the shape of lions' heads.

Tiny coves dot the coastline

Canyoning ★★

Not for the faint-hearted, canyoning involves launching yourself down a river or stream, over chutes and waterfalls – no kayaks or rafts are involved! Trips from Kaş head into the Kaputaş Canyon 20 km (12 miles) west of town.

Sea kayaking ★★★

You can travel to Üçağız for a day of kayaking in the azure waters of Kekova Sound (see page 72), with time to explore Kayaköy and the ancient remains of the Sunken City at closer quarters than on a tour boat. No experience needed.

Trekking ★

Kaş is right at the heart of the Lycian Way walking trail (see page 102). You can book guided walks for short sections close to the town to learn more about the history, flora and fauna of the region.

Swimming with dolphins ★★

The **Dolphin Therapy Centre** offers the opportunity to swim with these fabulous mammals (see Excursions, page 58).

Spa & Turkish baths ★

The **Phellos Health Club** has a modern hamam and spa for relaxation and massage. ⓐ Dogru Yol Sokak ⓣ 0242 836 1953 ❗ Admission charge

BEACHES

The beaches here are poor compared to resorts in the west of the Lycian region, and most swimming is from the coastal rocks or in artificial lidos.

Küçük Çakıl ★

The town beach is small, but is backed by hotels that can supply any refreshments you might need.

AGENCIES FOR ACTIVITIES

Bougainville Travel This English/Turkish company offers a full range of tours, but is respected for its activity-based excursions including canyoning, mountain biking, paragliding and trekking. ⓐ Çukurbağlı Caddesi 10 ⓣ 0242 836 3737 ⓦ www.bougainville-turkey.com

Dolce Vita This rival company offers similar day tours, plus day trips to Kaştellorizo (see page 46). ⓐ Cumhuriyet Meydani 7 ⓣ 0242 836 1610 ⓦ www.dolcevitatravel.org

Büyük Çakıl ★

A pebble beach that again, is not big, but is busy because of its relatively easy walk from town. ⓐ 1.5 km (1 mile) east of town

Kaputaş Beach ★★★

This small beach is reached by car or small boat. Its dramatic setting at the mouth of a high gorge makes it a popular spot for sunbathers and yachts. There are few facilities here, so it is best to bring a picnic. ⓐ 20 km (12 miles) west of town

EXCURSIONS

Day trips to Kastellorizo ★

Lying tantalizingly close to the shoreline – it looks like you could throw a stone to it, but is actually about three nautical miles – is the Greek island of **Kastellorizo**, also known in Greek as Megisti and in Turkish as Meis.

A remote outpost of the Dodecanese Islands (the same group as Rhodes and Kos), it was wealthy throughout the 19th century as a centre of shipbuilding and trade in high-quality sponges. There are some fine patrician mansions built by the leading families of the day on the waterfront of the main town, though many of these have a rather faded and careworn feel. There's a 14th-century castle of the Knights of St John and a small town museum. There was once an ancient site here, but the stones have been reused for the castle and the Church of Sts Constantine and Helena, erected in the 19th century. There are companies running day trips to the island from the harbour at Kaş (see box on page 45).

The Elmalı Plains ★

If you rent a car or hire a taxi for the day, it is worth heading inland. Once you climb up and over the **Ak Dağlar Mountains** that hem Kaş into the coastline, you reach a totally different landscape – a rich, fertile plain famed for its apple crops. In spring the air is heady with apple blossom, and early October sees the fruit harvested.

SHOPPING

Although it is a small resort, Kaş has some of the most interesting and unusual shopping opportunities along the Turkish coast. This is partly a legacy of its old hippy days, but also because it is a high-class resort attracting wealthy Turks with money to spend. The old mansions in the main streets have been converted into boutiques selling locally designed high-quality clothing, jewellery, antiques and, of course, carpets. It is a very atmospheric place to shop, especially in the evenings.

These individual boutiques have been joined by European high-street names – genuine here – such as Benetton and NafNaf.

There is also a bustling **Friday market** (see map on page 43).

You'll need a four-wheel drive vehicle to reach **Green Lake** high in the arid hills, as the steep road skirts the side of the hill and the surface is very loose. The lake, which was once a pilgrimage site, can totally dry up in summer, but the vistas are worth the trip. The small stone buildings on the plateau were seasonal shelters for shepherds who used to tend the herds here in summer.

Gömbe makes an interesting stop with its traditional local market, while **Sütleğan** sits at 1500 m (5000 ft) surrounded by mature pines and mountain scenery.

The town of **Elmalı** is low-key and not at all touristy. It has an interesting old quarter filled with cobbled lanes lined with Ottoman mansions plus a 17th-century mosque.

There are local dolmuş services to **Xanthos** (see page 80), **Letoön** (see page 75), **Fethiye** (see page 18), **Kalkan** (see page 34) and **Kale/Demre** (see page 78).

Spices at the market

RESTAURANTS **(see map on page 43)**

Bahçe €–€€ ❶ Excellent *meze* here, with traditional decor and a garden. Uzun Çarşi Caddesi (next to the Lion Tomb) 0242 836 2370 Open 11.00–15.00 and 18.00–midnight

Café Merhaba € ❷ Enjoy a good book with coffee and home-made cakes here, an informal meeting place with souvenirs. Ibrahim Serin Caddesi 0242 836 1883 Open 07.00–16.00

Chez Evi €€€ ❸ In the 1980s, French *cordon-bleu*-trained Evi chose Kaş as her new home, and now Chez Evi is a little piece of 'ooh la la' in Turkey. The food is authentic and delicious, including dishes such as crepe suzette or coq au vin. ⓐ Terzi Sokak 2 ⓣ 0242 836 1253 ⓒ Open daily 18.00–23.00 (summer); Tues–Sat 18.00–21.00 (winter)

Noel Baba Pastanesi € ❹ An old-fashioned Turkish pastry house that has now expanded its menu to include savoury snacks. This place has long been popular with locals and is one of the best places in Kaş to watch the world go by, whatever the time of day. ⓐ Cumhuriyet Meydani 14 (the main square) ⓣ 0242 836 1225 ⓒ Open 08.00–01.00

Oba Restaurant € ❺ A little out of the mainstream, up the hill in town, Oba serves authentic and good value *meze,* plus a range of vegetarian main dishes. They cook fresh every day and you'll need to visit the kitchen to decide what you want. ⓐ Çukurbağlı Caddesi ⓣ 0242 836 1687 ⓒ Open 11.00–midnight

NIGHTLIFE

Harry's Bar ❻ One of Kaş's trendy bars, with a friendly but relaxed welcome, where everyone gathers for an early- or late-evening drink. ⓐ Ibrahim Serin Caddesi 13 ⓣ 0242 836 1379 ⓒ Open 11.00–03.00

Hi Jazz ❼ Great live jazz every evening with a repertoire that features everything from classical to improvisation. The performances build through the evening, so come early for some gentle accompaniment to your pre-dinner drink or after-dinner for some stomping sounds. ⓐ Zumrut Sokak 3 ⓣ 0242 836 1165 ⓒ Open 19.00–03.00

Mavi Bar ❽ This bar has remained a constant feature of the Kaş scene for the last few years. It is a relaxed café/bar with outdoor seating and a great view of the main square and waterfront. ⓐ Cumhuriyet Meydani (the main square) ⓒ Open 09.00–03.00

Turunç
a perfect horseshoe bay

Set in a dramatic cove surrounded by craggy bluffs, Turunç (pronounced *Turunch*) is a picturesque resort, with its curved golden beach and hotels and *pensiyons* dotted around the pine-clad hills. There is still an air of exclusivity here as you drop into the resort, leaving the noise and bustle of Marmaris behind to find a slower, gentler pace of life.

Whilst Turunç is not for those who want to be in the centre of the action, you can still link up with any excursion that travels from the larger resort. It is perfect for those who want a medium-sized resort, but with the possibility of dipping into Turkey's most energetic beach and nightlife.

Although the surrounding hills and coves hide the remains of many ancient settlements, the resort itself doesn't have a long history, developing as a small fishing village before eventually moving into tourism.

THINGS TO SEE & DO

Boat trips ★★

There are regular boat taxis to Turunç's bustling sister resort of **Marmaris**. Most people also spend at least one day enjoying a boat taxi trip to the beaches of the peaceful neighbouring bays. The Five-Bays trip is the most popular from the harbour at Turunç, out into the **Bay of Marmaris**, including the famous **Cleopatra Island** (see page 13).

Walks ★

The whole of the **Bozburun** peninsula is excellent for walking and hiking, and there are a number of marked paths leading from the resort. The bay of **Amos** is about an hour's walk along the coast road, with **Kumlubük** about 30 minutes further on. Alternatively, head into the hills, just remember to take some water and to wear suitable strong footwear.

The dramatic cove of Turunç

Outdoor activities ★★★

Erokoy Tours offer a range of sporting activities, from horse riding through the pine forests to sea kayaking in the calm bays. ⓐ Kayabal Caddesi 40, Içmeler ⓣ 0252 455 5522 ⓦ www.anatoliandiscovery.com

BEACHES

The town beach is a beautiful curved sand and shingle strand – one of the best in the area – but for that reason it can be very busy with boat trippers from Marmaris. The shallow incline makes it good for children and non-swimmers, and the water sports opportunities are good.

For a little more peace and quiet, head to **Kumlubük** around the bay. Much of the land here is privately owned by one man, so you don't get many hotels and apartments and can escape the crowds.

EXCURSIONS

Ancient Amos ★

Amos is an ancient Rhodian and Hellenistic settlement and once had a population of 15,000 people. Today there remains little more than parts of the Acropolis, a temple, an untidy theatre and a few sections of wall. However, the beautiful views across the water with its sprinkling of islands and inlets make the trip worthwhile, and you'll probably have the place to yourself.

Around the Bozburun Peninsula ★

The Bozburun peninsula south of the resort is the perfect place for exploration with a rental car. Here you will find tiny coastal villages in which to enjoy a relaxing seafood lunch, plus the remains of ancient places such as Ceresse, Paridon, Saranda, Tymuns and, at the very southern tip, Loryma.

RESTAURANTS

Çinar Restaurant € A great choice for good-value Turkish cuisine, Çinar is at the heart of the resort, so you can watch the world go by. ⓐ Sokak 22 ⓣ 0252 7123 ⓛ Open 11.00–midnight

The shallow, shingle beach at Turunç is perfect for children

Musti's Restaurant €€ Good value for money in the heart of the resort, Musti's serves standard grilled meats and steaks plus Greek-influenced dishes like *kleftiko* (slow-cooked lamb). ⓐ H Mustafa Can Caddesi ⓣ 0252 476 7084 ⓛ Open 08.00–midnight

NIGHTLIFE

Habit Bar This family-run bar is where everybody meets early or late in the evening. Cihan, the owner, does great cocktails. Food is also available, so you could spend all evening here. ⓐ H Mustafa Can Caddesi ⓣ 0252 476 7581 ⓛ Open 11.00–03.00

Içmeler
sheltered beach resort

Içmeler (pronounced ich-miller) sits in one of the most picturesque bays on the Bozburun peninsula to the west of Marmaris. It boasts a sheltered golden beach shaded by palm trees, backed by forested hills and looking out on numerous off-shore islands. It has developed fast since the early 1990s, but still has touches of the old ways of life, with traditional houses set amongst the modern hotels.

THINGS TO SEE & DO

Little Train ★

Really this is just another form of public transport to get holidaymakers around the resort, but it is a good way to get your bearings and one of the cheapest tours you can get.

Boat rides ★★

Take the water taxi to **Marmaris** (see pages 13–15). This is a great form of public transport that is worth taking just for the ride. It runs several times every day in peak season.

From the waterfront in town you have the same choice of trips as those available from Marmaris. Head to **Turunç** (see page 50) for a more low-key resort atmosphere, or to the south-west beyond Turunç for empty bays for great swimming and snorkelling.

SHOPPING

The canal that runs through Içmeler has shops along its length and is a particularly romantic place to shop in the evenings, when a ribbon of lights adds a golden glow. There is also a good market on Wednesdays, but Içmeler is so close to Marmaris and its amazing shopping opportunities that most people head there to spend their holiday cash!

The picturesque bay of Içmeler

Diving ★

Diver's Delight This company, which has been open since the late 1980s, runs 'Try-a-Dive' days and PADI qualification courses. ⓐ Kayabal Caddesi 63 ⓣ 0252 455 3885 ⓦ www.diversdelight.com

Spa & Turkish baths ★

Hotel Aqua This spa offers various massages, body wraps and aromatherapy treatments, plus ayurveda and yoga sessions for total relaxation. ⓐ Sahil Sokak 5 ⓣ 0252 455 3636 ⓦ www.hotelaqua.com

BEACHES

The resort beach of golden sand and small shingle runs around the bay, and there are several café bars right on the beach so you don't need to move far for lunch or drinks. There is also an ample selection of water sports – both motorized and non-motorized – to enjoy.

EXCURSIONS

You can easily get involved in any of the excursions from **Marmaris** (see page 16) and **Turunç** (see page 52).

RESTAURANTS

Golden Beach Restaurant €€ Directly on the beach and open throughout the day, Golden Beach offers a great venue for lunch, dinner or drinks, with views across the water. Live music every night from 20.00. ⓐ Altin Sahil ⓣ 0252 455 4670 Ⓛ Open 08.00–01.00

Majestic Restaurant €€ Voted best restaurant in town a number of times, the Majestic has a mixed menu including both European and Asian dishes. ⓐ Cumhuriyet Mah, Osman Gazi Caddesi 30 ⓣ 0252 455 2740 Ⓛ Open 11.00–02.00

Taj Mahal €€ If you can't do without your curry fix while on holiday, Taj Mahal offers a decent choice with authentic flavours and some vegetarian options. The chef is from Bradford, so you can't go wrong! ⓐ Corner Kenan Evran Bul and Istiklal Caddesi ⓣ 0252 455 4580 Ⓛ Open 17.00–midnight

NIGHTLIFE

Linekers This English-run sports bar is one of the longest-running venues in the resort. You can be sure of getting Premiership football games along with full cooked breakfasts and an evening meat carvery. There is disco music plus a swimming pool on site. Once you get here, you might not leave until it's time for your flight home! ⓐ Off Cumhuriyet Caddesi ⓣ 0252 455 5981 Ⓛ Open 08.00–03.00

Starlight Nights Unusual to see in Turkey, Starlight Nights offers Las Vegas-style revue shows (three shows to suit different age groups) with glamorous sequin-clad dancers. Dinner and your first drink is included in the price. Tickets are available through your holiday representative or tour agent in the resort. Ⓛ Open from 19.00 during the season

EXCURSIONS
Out & about

Lycian adventures

THINGS TO SEE & DO

Jeep or 4x4 safari ★★★

The jeep safari is a real adventure. Out and about on roads you'd never venture to in a rental car, it gives you a chance to see the traditional Turkish way of life and discover the countryside surrounding your resort. Routes vary with each company, but the following gives you an idea of where you might like to go.

In the mountains behind **Kaş**, you can tour the lands around the farming villages of **Ugrar**, **Sütleğan** and **Gökceören**, with a stop for lunch in a village house.

Fethiye has some excellent inland locations that are also easily reached from **Hisarönü** and **Ölüdeniz**. Ancient **Tlos** or the hills around **Baba Dağ** offer exciting overland journeys.

From Marmaris, Içmeler and Turunç, the **Hisarönü** and **Datça peninsula** are open to you. There are breathtaking unspoilt coves and forested hillsides (some areas are still recovering from devastating fires in the 1990s) to explore. Very sparsely populated, the countryside provides a lovely contrast to the busy resorts.

Swimming with dolphins ★★★

The **Dolphin Therapy Centre** has been running carefully supervised programmes for children with mental and physical disabilities in conjunction with a medical institute in Russia. This work is still carrying on, but now the centre is also running swim-with-the-dolphins sessions for the public. You can spend 15–20 minutes in the water with a bottlenose dolphin or simply watch the activities from the viewing gantry if you do not want to swim. The centre is situated in Kaş, but the ticket agent is in Fethiye and runs transport from there to Kaş. This means that the excursion is easy to join from other resorts, such as Ölüdeniz, Hisarönü and Fethiye, as well as Kaş and Kalkan.

Contact **Gala Yachting & Travel** ⓐ Cumhuriyet Mah, Sokak 503, Fethiye ⓣ 0252 614 0308 ⓦ www.dolphintherapycenter.com

Paragliding ★★★

One of the most awe-inspiring and exhilarating ways to experience the Turkish coast is by being strapped to a qualified paraglider and jumping off a Lycian mountain. Don't worry, you will be given some instruction about what to do before you take the leap of faith, then you will be guided down in a journey that lasts over an hour. Two areas to try are:

Mount Baba If you are staying in Ölüdeniz, Hisarönü or Fethiye, try the trip from the summit of Mount Baba above Ölüdeniz. This is the longest paragliding drop in the world, at 1900 m (3250 ft). You will spiral down over the teardrop beach and its limpid lagoon, but not before you've enjoyed the staggering long-distance views. Contact **Sky Sports** in Ölüdeniz. ⓣ 0252 617 0511 ⓦ www.skysports-turkey.com

Mount Asaz There is a launch area close to the summit of Mount Asaz, near Kaş, with a 1000 m (3300 ft) drop. The descent offers incredible views over the Lycian coastline and across to the island of Kaştellorizo just off shore, before landing back in the centre of Kaş just by the harbour. **Bougainville Travel** (see page 45) organizes jumps.

Your normal travel insurance does not cover you for tandem paragliding, so make sure you choose a reputable company with good insurance.

Microlighting ★★★

If you'd rather take an aerial tour of the **Ölüdeniz** area under the power of an engine than simply under a parachute, try microlighting. These small, manoeuvrable craft offer you a bird's-eye view over the mountains and off shore, but you sit in a seat at the side of a qualified pilot rather than dangling from a harness. **Fly South** offer flights from the runway at Hisarönü. ⓘ Book with your holiday representative or a local agency.

Whitewater rafting on the Dalaman River ★

This is just about the most energetic and exhilarating activity you can find along the Turkish coast. Dalaman River rafting is world famous for its challenging grade four rapids. However, many sections are not very difficult, so if you are a rafting virgin it is the perfect place to start. There is enough white water here to get your adrenalin rushing, but plenty of quiet spells in between for you to catch your breath and take in the wonderful views.

The journey to the rafting departure point (1.5 hours from Fethiye or Marmaris) is also spectacular, with a route through the **Taurus Mountains** offering dramatic landscapes and a glimpse of rural lifestyles.

The large rafts can carry about 15 people, so they are perfect for a group. You will get a guide to show you the basics and will be kitted out with all the necessary safety gear. Then there will be a bit of singing to get you in the party mood before it's 'paddles at the ready'. All the rafts stay together on the river and the guides are on hand to make sure the trip is safe and fun.

The rafting starts quietly before leading through several sections of rapids with names like Rockgate, Long Rapid, Slingshot and Nazaretme, where you'll need to use all your new-found skills.

All this excitement really builds an appetite, so you will appreciate the simple lunch of barbecued meats and delicious fresh trout plus salads and fruit to build up your energy levels again.

After swimming in the rock pools or a spot of sunbathing, you will carry on down the river, under the ancient Roman bridge, before reaching the village of **Akkopru**, the end of the trip.

The travel company **Alternatif Turizam** in Marmaris run well-organized rafting tours, with pick-ups from along the Lycian coast. They also offer river and sea kayaking, canyoning, hiking and mountain biking. ⓐ Camlik Sokak 10/1 ⓣ 0252 417 2720

Children under six years of age are not allowed to ride in the rafts for safety reasons.

Saklıkent Gorge

A dramatic landscape feature, Saklıkent Gorge cuts 18 km (11 miles) into the Akdağlar Mountains, carved by the power of water and wind.

HIGHLIGHTS

Saklıkent Gorge floor ★

You can walk for 2 km (1.2 miles) along the gorge floor. Any further exploration requires ropes and climbing equipment! There is a metal walkway along the first 150 m (165 yd) where the gorge is at its widest, and you'll reach a shady restaurant by the water's edge. From here you have to paddle through the freezing water to reach the gorge floor. The sheer walls are curved into all sorts of surreal shapes. In certain places you'll have to climb through narrow boulder-strewn gaps and rock pools.

At the mouth of the gorge there are several restaurants by the river with wooden verandas overhanging the water. This is a wonderfully atmospheric place to enjoy a drink or a lunch of fresh trout (farmed nearby). ⓐ 40 km (25 miles) east of Fethiye 🕒 Open sunrise–sunset ❗ Admission charge

TURKISH EVENING

Genuine Turkish food and entertainment may be difficult to find in many modern resorts, but the 'Turkish evening' offers the perfect introduction to the culture and it's a really fun evening out. You'll start with a buffet meal of *meze* dishes, barbecued meats and salads, washed down with local wine or beer (see page 92 for more details of traditional foods). After dinner you will be entertained by a troupe performing local folkloric dances plus of course the famous belly dance, regarded by the Ottomans as the height of eroticism. Someone from the audience is always invited to have a go, which is usually hilarious. Later in the evening, the dance floor is handed over to the guests for an hour or so of disco dancing.

Rhodes Town

The Greek island of Rhodes is one of the jewels of the eastern Mediterranean. Its unique old town makes an interesting day trip, most easily taken from Marmaris, or from much of the western region.

HISTORY

The immense citadel of Rhodes Town was the headquarters of the Knights of St John from 1309. The knights provided medical care for pilgrims on journeys to the Holy Land, but later became one of the leading medieval military organizations and the front line against the forces of Islam coming from the East. In 1522, after a long siege, Ottoman forces took Rhodes and held it until 1912. Following the Italian–Turkish War, the island was ceded to Italy. It then became part of Greece in 1947.

THINGS TO SEE & DO

The town walls ★★★

The high sandstone walls are 4 km (2.5 miles) long. Seven of the original eight gates still remain in use today, the most interesting being the **d'Amboise Gate** in the north-west corner, built in 1512. This curves in an 'S' shape to outwit attackers and is linked to a second gate, **St Anthony's**, which lies between two inner curtain walls. The **Sea Gate**, closest to the port, is the most impressive, flanked by two massive round towers. A walk around the walls takes approximately 40 minutes.

The Knights' Quarter or Collachium ★★★

The old town is divided into two sectors: the Collachium, where the knights lived, and the Chora, where the rest of the population lived. The Collachium dates back to 1309 and is a good place to begin.

Panagía tou Kástrou (The Church of Our Lady of the Castle) ★

This 14th-century building used to be the knight's cathedral. It was converted into a mosque during the Ottoman period and local Rhodians call it the Red Church because of massacres that took place inside when the Muslims arrived. Today it is home to the **Museum of Religious Art in the Post-Byzantine Period**, displaying a collection of icons from the 14th, 15th and 20th centuries. Ⓐ Platía Moussíou (Museum Square) Ⓛ Open Tues–Sun 08.30–15.00 ❶ Admission charge

Archaeological Museum of Rhodes ★★★

The museum is housed in the 15th-century Knights' Hospital. The medieval building was state-of-the-art for its time. Inside, **The Infirmary Room** houses relics of the era of the knights, with gravestones and coats of arms of illustrious members on display.

The rest of the rooms display ancient statuary and other artefacts from various Dodecanese islands, many of which were excavated during the Italian Period. The grave *stele* of Krito and Tamerista, carved around 410 BC by a local artist, is one of the most renowned exhibits. Ⓐ Platía Moussíou Ⓛ Open Mon noon–19.00 and Tues–Sun 08.00–19.00 (Apr–Oct); Tues–Sun 09.30–15.00 (Nov–Mar) ❶ Admission charge.

Odós Ippotón (Street of the Knights) ★★★

This is one of the most complete medieval streets in the world, with a long facade of fine, carved stonemasonry on which many small details

The walled city of Rhodes Town

can be seen. The **Inn of France** is the most highly decorated and its internal courtyard has a chapel dating from *c.* 1374, though the street frontage dates from over 100 years later.

Palace of the Grand Master ★★★

This was the administrative heart and power base of the Order of the Knights of St John. Dating from the late 15th century, it was badly damaged by an explosion in 1856 and was renovated by the Italians.

The ground floor rooms, which originally acted as stables and grain and munitions stores, are reached across a courtyard sporting a series of classical statues. They house a permanent exhibition of finds from 2400 years of Rhodes' history, plus other temporary exhibitions. Many of the major rooms on the upper floors have beautiful Hellenistic, Roman and early-Christian mosaics taken from the neighbouring island of Kos. These include one depicting the nine muses and another showing the head of the Medusa. Though it is ethically questionable whether they should be here, they have been carefully preserved and look spectacular. ⓐ Top of Odós Ippotón ⓑ Mon noon–19.00 and Tues–Sun 08.00–19.00 (Jul–Oct); Tues–Sun 09.30–15.00 (Nov–June) ⓘ Admission charge

The Chora or Town ★★★

The Knights lived in the Collachium, but a thriving town developed within the city walls and much of this remains as it was during the Ottoman era. This quarter is a maze of stone alleyways, some bustling, others deserted. Stone archways spanning the lanes add a particular character and also serve the serious function of providing structural support during earthquakes. Take your time to explore here – streets such as Fanouriou, Pithagora and Sophocleous make good starting points.

Mosque of Suleyman ★

Built in 1523 to mark the Ottoman takeover of the island, the mosque has recently been renovated. Climb the small flight of steps at the back for the best views of the large dome that tops the building. ⓐ Odós Panetiou ⓘ Not open to the public

To Roloi ★★★

Climb to the top of this clock tower, erected in 1851, for impressive views over the rooftops of the Old Town. From here you can clearly see what a maze it is. Ⓐ Odós Panetiou Ⓒ Open 08.00–22.00 Ⓘ Admission charge

Odós Sokratous (Socrates Street) ★★★

The main shopping thoroughfare in Ottoman times, Odós Sokratous, is at first glance, just as it was 150 years ago, thronging with people bargaining for goods in many languages and shopkeepers willing to do a little bartering to secure a sale. Of course, times have changed – the constant ring of mobile phones reminds you that you're in the 21st century.

Platía Ippokrátous (Hippocrates Square) ★★

One of the main meeting places in the Old Town, Platía Ippokrátous, is decorated by a Sintrivani fountain, topped by a miniature minaret. In the south-eastern corner of the square, the stone building called the **Castellenia** (completed in 1507) was the medieval courthouse and stock exchange. It now houses the public library and town archives.

Platía Evréon Martyron (Square of the Martyrs) ★

This square is named in remembrance of the 2000 people who lived in Rhodes Town when the Germans arrived in 1943 after Italian capitulation, of whom only 50 returned after the war. On the north side of the square are the old Naval Headquarters for the knights, which became the seat of the Christian Orthodoxy Church in Rhodes, now known as the **Archbishop's Palace**. The 16th-century **Kal de Shalom Synagogue** has been carefully renovated. Ⓐ Odós Dosaidou, just off the square.

RESTAURANTS

Taverna Kostas €–€€€ Off the beaten tourist track on an old, narrow street, Taverna Kostas has been run by the same family for over 30 years. It is popular with locals for its authentic cuisine. Relax in the lovely terrace garden over a meal or a snack. Ⓐ Odós Pythagora 62 Ⓣ 0241 26217 Ⓒ Open all year 11.00–15.00 and 18.00–late Ⓘ Cash only

Antalya

The anchor city of the Mediterranean coast, Antalya is, aside from Istanbul, the most 'happening' city in the country, and it is the perfect place to capture the 'East meets West' clash of cultures that encapsulates modern Turkey.

HISTORY

The Persians founded Antalya in 158 BC on the site of a deep natural harbour. It was important throughout ancient times and came to be prized by the Romans and Byzantines because it was safe and gave them easy access to the whole eastern Mediterranean.

When the Ottomans took over the city in the 16th century, it was surrounded by a 5 km (3 mile) long wall. They divided the city into four districts, each housing the Greek, Jewish and Muslim communities, and also the ruling classes or Mamelukes.

After the fall of the Ottoman Empire, the city was abandoned and its mansions became dilapidated, but since the 1980s it has undergone a huge programme of renovation and has been reborn as the largest medieval citadel along the Turkish tourist coast.

THINGS TO SEE & DO

Antalya Beach Park ★★★

A fantastic concept for a city resort, Antalya Beach Park to the west of the downtown core is a huge pre-planned leisure area with a range of activities and some lovely natural areas to explore. There is a paintball arena, golf, parks and children's play areas, a range of food from snack kiosks to restaurants, plus access to Konyaaltı Beach for water sports. The two major attractions are: **Aqualand**, a huge waterpark with impressive rides with names like Twister and Black Hole, a massive wave pool and a kids play area; and **Dolphinland**, where you can watch the dolphin shows and even have the opportunity to swim with the dolphins.
ⓐ Dumlupinar Bul. Konyaaltı Korulugu Yani ⓣ 0242 249 0900
ⓦ www.beachpark.com.tr

Aqualand water park is a must for kids

Antalya Archaeological Museum ★★★

This is one of the best museums of ancient finds in the eastern Mediterranean. Even if you don't normally enjoy tramping around ancient ruins, you will be impressed by the amazing artefacts on display here. These have been brought from sites all around the Turkish Mediterranean.

The highlight of the museum is the collection of artefacts from the **ancient city of Perge** to the east of Antalya. This highly decorated, monumental statuary (mostly 2nd century AD) shows just how sophisticated the city must have been in its heyday. Look particularly for a beautiful statue of a dancer carved using two different marbles – her light skin contrasting with her dark hair and dress. The collection of ornamental friezes that decorated the theatre at Perge is considered the finest of its type in the world.

The star of the museum's **Byzantine and Christian collection** is the reliquary that is said to have held the bones of the 4th-century AD Bishop of Myra, St Nicholas (or Baba Noel as he is known in Turkish), the saint on whom the modern legend of Santa Claus is based (see page 79). The collection also includes icons recovered from various churches after the Greek community left in the 1920s.

The museum also houses **Bronze Age finds** which include items from the 6th–8th centuries BC, when the Phrygian people inhabited the area. The best include statuary and funerary urns.

The most interesting area in this **ethnological collection** of Selçuk and Ottoman handicrafts is the diorama of a traditional nomadic lifestyle, showing how many Turks lived until the 20th century, and some still do. ⓐ Cumhuriyet Caddesi ● Open Tues–Sun 09.00–18.00, closed Mon ● Admission charge

Kaleiçi (Old Quarter) ★★★

This medieval labyrinth of narrow alleyways and courtyarded mansions is still evocative of Ottoman Turkey, though its history dates back to before Roman times. Today the quarter is home to stylish boutique hotels, upmarket restaurants and bohemian shops.

There is no set route for sightseeing, just follow your nose around the next picture-perfect corner, browsing as you go. You will be able to explore excellent renovations and evocative ruins, but whether the mansion is a palace or the pits, the beauty is in the detail – wooden lintels, stone archways and a palate of weather-worn pastel stucco walls add to the atmosphere. Look out for the following highlights on your wanders around the old town:

City walls Various sections of the Roman city wall survive. At Kalekapısı, the main entrance to Kaleiçi, a section of wall supports Saat Kulesi, a Selçuk clock tower. Other sections run from the harbour around the rocky coastline, but the longest and most impressive stretch runs south of Hadrian's Gate (see below).

Yivli Minare (Fluted Minaret) Built in 1230 by Sultan Alâeddin Keykubad, the fluted mosque, so called because the minaret has a fluted tower, has become a symbol of Antalya. The mosque next door is still used for worship.

Hadrian's Gate Built at the eastern flank of Roman Antalya in AD 130, this triumphal arch celebrated a visit to the city by Emperor Hadrian. A flight of steps leading down to the gate shows just how much higher the modern city is than it was in Roman times.

The old harbour Down on the shore below the mansions of Kaleiçi, the harbour is now a pleasure marina with a flotilla of little boats offering tours of the bay. There are several cafés and restaurants, so it is a popular place for lunch. While you are relaxing, you can examine the walls of the harbour, which were built by the Romans and have been reinforced regularly since then.

RESTAURANTS

Anfi €€ Also in the harbour area, this is a very popular restaurant with the locals because it serves excellent food at reasonable prices. Try the *meze* dishes. It also has a large terrace. ⓐ Kaleiçi Yat Limani (in the old port) ⓣ 0242 243 2073 ⓑ Open 11.00–midnight

Dalyan boat trip

The Dalyan boat trip is one of most fun-filled excursions you can take and it brings everything that's great about a holiday in Turkey – a little bit of history, fantastic views, lots of wildlife, swimming and mud baths – together in one action-packed day.

Dalyan Çayı (Dalyan River) drains freshwater Köyceğiz Gölü (Lake Köyceğiz) and runs into the Mediterranean. The slow-moving river meanders between two high limestone bluffs, and its banks are lined with thick reed beds that support a wealth of bird life, such as storks and herons, plus fish and amphibians. As in ancient times there are several fish farms along the banks and delicious freshly grilled trout is a delicacy of the region. Daily tours at 10.30 from Dalyan river docks, returning at 16.00 Admission charge (plus separate charge for Kaunos site and mud baths)

BOAT TRIP SIGHTS

Lycian tombs ★★★

Across the river from Dalyan village is an impressive collection of Lycian tombs. They are numerous and incredibly elegantly carved, but most awe-inspiring is the fact that they sit high up on the cliff side with no obvious means of access, prompting the question – how did the ancient Lycians carve out the tombs without the aid of modern scaffolding?

Kaunos ★

These magnificent cliff tombs were the work of the people of ancient Kaunos. During ancient times, the city sat above a malaria-infested swamp (mosquitoes can still be a problem here but the malaria has been eradicated) and was said to be one of the most unhealthy places in the Roman Empire. The city made money from the ancient slave trade until the river silted up and the docks could no longer operate.

Most of the city hasn't been excavated. There are regular digs during the summer but progress is slow. The site offers excellent views out over the valley and along the river to the sea, which is now 5 km (3 miles) away. This is probably the highlight of the tour – especially if ancient remains aren't your thing.

The lower town has a Roman baths complex plus temples and an agora. The Acropolis has evidence of fortifications from the 3rd century BC to medieval times, plus a well-preserved Hellenistic theatre.

It is a 10-minute walk from the boat dock to the remains, and the route is steep in parts, so wear comfortable shoes and take some water with you.

İztuzu Beach ★★

Your river trip continues seaward, where the next stop is **İztuzu Beach**, a spectacular 7 km (4.4 mile) swathe of sand backed by scrub-covered dunes, whose western advance is narrowing the river's mouth. İztuzu is a major turtle-nesting beach and you may spot one of these shy creatures in the shallows during the laying season between May and July.

Since these creatures are now endangered, please follow the guidelines to protect the nests. These are printed on panels around the site. The most important of these is not to enter the taped-off area where the eggs are located.

The sea here can have quite high waves because the bay is open to the prevailing winds, but the marshes behind the dunes have warm calm pools, much more suited for swimming. These are also home to lots of wildlife species, including fantastic iridescent dragonflies, terrapins and the now rare Anatolian tortoise.

Ilıca mud baths ★★

Said to be beneficial for rheumatism and male potency, most holidaymakers visit for the fun of smearing themselves in the warm brown goo!

Lake Köyceğiz ★

On the return journey to Dalyan, boats rest at Lake Köyceğiz and you can swim in the cool, fresh water.

Kekova boat trip

The coastal shallows of Kekova Sound in south-east Lycia make one of the most beautiful and popular day trips along this part of the coast. Kekova Island shelters crystal-clear waters and numerous rocky islets. The vista is topped off by the jagged, arid Lycian peaks just inland.

Until recently, this idyllic corner of the Turkish coast was the exclusive preserve of 'yachties' who could lay anchor in one of the many remote coves seemingly miles away from the rest of the world. Today, the pleasures of the area can be enjoyed by everyone for a lot less than the cost of a yacht charter – and with lunch included in the package.
Boat trips daily (weather permitting in winter) Admission charge (plus a charge for entering the castle)

Boat trips set off from all parts of the coast, east and west. The further you travel in the boat, the less time you'll have at Kekova, so you may not experience all the activities listed below. The itinerary here assumes that you have sailed from the closest port, Üçağız.

BOAT TRIP SIGHTS

Kekova Island ★★

Kekova Island lies just a few hundred metres off shore and only became an island when the level of the Mediterranean rose in the early part of the first millennium. As the water flooded in, it swallowed the ancient city that thrived here. The city remains are called Batıkent (the 'sunken city') but archaeologists haven't yet identified which city it actually was.

The island is protected as an ancient site so no one is allowed to set foot on it, but your boat will get in close to shore and you can get good views of the remains of numerous stone buildings clinging to the hillside, and the ancient harbour just below the waterline. Under the water are the remains of yet more buildings, and the seabed is dotted with ancient pottery amphora lying where they fell many hundreds of years ago.

The necropolis of Teimiussa ★

On the inland shoreline are the remains of ancient Teimiussa, half-submerged in water and half-choked by the fertile mud that now helps make this part of Turkey the capital of fruit and vegetable production. Look out particularly for several excellent Lycian tombs rising out of the water, supported on their stone pillars.

Kaleköy ★★★

Kaleköy (the ancient site of Simena) is one of the prettiest and most authentic villages along the Turkish coast, and the view as you approach from the water makes a perfect picture with a rash of traditional whitewashed houses climbing up the hillside, crowned by a sturdy fortress (see below).

Once your boat has moored at one of the numerous rustic wooden jetties, you are free to explore the narrow winding alleyways. The settlement is a fascinating mixture of living community and tourist town. Most of the houses are family homes and chickens roam free throughout the village, scattering noisily as you approach. The older women sit in their doorways crocheting or making the lace that is on sale everywhere; children offer fruit or small trinkets, while carpet shops simply hang their wares off balconies or over walls.

The Fortress of the Knights of St John ★★

The fortress was built by the Knights of St John and offers wonderful high-level views over Kekova sound and the town. It's one of their smaller outposts but still a beautiful example of crusader architecture.
🕒 24 hours ❗ Admission charge when guardian is on duty

Swimming ★

After your explorations, you will be allowed time for swimming and snorkelling. Watch out for the spiny sea urchins that breed in the shallows here. If you step on them, the spines break off in your foot and can become infected.

Letoön harbour

Letoön

Lycia's most important religious site, Letoön, was home to the shrine of the Lycians' major goddess Leto. It was also the site of a famed Oracle and played host to festivals organized by the cities that made up the Lycian Federation (one of the world's earliest democratic governments).

When Alexander the Great arrived in Letoön in 334 BC, the Oracle informed him that his forces would crush the Persians, which is just what they went on to do (and far more). Under the Romans, the shrine remained an important place of pilgrimage. Later, under the Byzantines, it was converted into a Christian basilica and thrived until Arab raiders pillaged the area in the 7th century. Charles Fellows discovered the site during his explorations of the 1840s but thankfully moved on to Xanthos (see page 80) to strip that city of its finest treasures. Letoön was only seriously excavated in the 1960s.

The site consists mainly of the remains of various temples. At the centre is a trio dedicated to Leto, Artemis and Apollo – the three major deities of the Lycians. The temple of Apollo has a fine mosaic floor featuring a lyre and a bow and arrow (symbolizing Artemis and Apollo). Open 08.00–19.30 (summer); 08.00–17.00 (winter)
Admission charge

LETO'S STORY

Leto was a water nymph who caught the eye of Zeus (head of the Greek gods) and they embarked on a passionate affair. Leto became pregnant but was discovered by Zeus' wife, Hera, who banished her. As she wandered the countryside to find somewhere to give birth to the twins Apollo and Artemis, she found a spring on the site of Letoön, but was shunned by local herdsmen. Eventually she was led to drink at the River Xanthos by a family of wolves. The Greek word *lykos* – the derivation of Lycia – means wolf.

Tlos

Normally linked with Saklıkent Gorge (see page 61) on a day trip from the coast, Tlos was one of the Lycian Federation's most important cities.

The site has a magnificent setting, but it hasn't been excavated and archaeologists still aren't sure what all the buildings are. ⓐ 22 km (14 miles) from Fethiye ◷ 24 hours ⓘ Admission charge if ticket collector present

HIGHLIGHTS

The baths complex ★

With its section of five-arched windows, this is one of the most complete sections of stonework at the site.

The theatre ★

With its backdrop of Lycian peaks, this is very atmospheric and has some finely carved seating still intact.

Tomb of Bellerophon ★★

Set amongst a series of Lycian rock-cut tombs is the so-called Bellerophon Tomb, a large and impressive example with a temple-style facade and a

THE STORY OF BELLEROPHON

Bellerophon was wrongly accused by King Proteus of making advances towards his Queen. He was ordered to visit the land of neighbouring Iobates, King of Lycia, with a note saying 'kill this subject of mine'.

Iobates could not kill the boy outright but sent him on a series of supposedly impossible missions. However, when Bellerophon completed all the tasks asked of him, Iobates decided to tell him of the message and to take Bellerophon as an ally. When Iobates died, Bellerophon became King of Lycia.

The ancient theatre of Tlos

bas-relief depicting Bellerophon riding Pegasus, the winged horse. One of the ruling families of the city claimed descent from the mythical hero Bellerophon and archaeologists assume this is their royal tomb.

Ottoman fortification ★

To the right of the site as you approach, look for some fortifications that were built in the Ottoman era by a feudal-style ruler Ali Ağa, nicknamed 'Bloody' by the local population who suffered under his patronage.

Myra & Kale

The site at ancient Myra allows you to get up close to some of the best Lycian tombs in Turkey. The modern town of Kale (also known locally as Demre) close to the site has been a centre of pilgrimage for many centuries because it is the birthplace of St Nicholas – our Santa Claus or, as he is known in Turkey, Baba Noel.

HIGHLIGHTS

Dating back to the 5th century BC, Myra was one of the most important cities of the ancient Lycian people. It supplied a form of incense to the expanding Greek and Roman world. The city was finally abandoned after earthquake damage and much of the site is still to be excavated. Today there are three main areas to explore.

The Sea Necropolis ★★★

The main collection of tombs, known as the Sea Necropolis are carved at eye level into the sheer cliff face. The tombs were carved to imitate the house of the subject during life, with an ornate door marking the entrance. Unlike at Dalyan (see page 70), you can get up close to the carvings to study the detail, but you can't go inside.

The theatre ★★

Next to the tombs is a well-preserved theatre, one of the smallest at a major site in Turkey. The entrance galleries and stairs used by Roman audiences are still pretty much intact, so you can climb them and imagine you are going to take your seat for an ancient play. There are good views towards the sea from its vaulted upper walkway. The decorative friezes of theatrical muse masks that once framed the stage now lie scattered across the site.

The River Necropolis ★★

A less-visited group of tombs can be found to the right of the theatre, a 10-minute walk through farmland from the main road.

Known as the River Necropolis because it faces the river (usually dried up in summer), the most important tomb here is known as the Painted Tomb. When it was first discovered by explorers in the 1840s, the tomb was covered in bright pigment, but this has since disappeared. Even so, the reliefs depicting a Lycian family group are still impressive.

Baba Noel Kilesi (The Church of St Nicholas) ★★★

Baba Noel Kilesi (The Church of St Nicholas) was built in the 8th century to house the body of the saint (which was later lost during a pirate raid in the 11th century).

The church is an excellent example of the Byzantine or Romanesque style. Decorated with beautiful inlaid patterned floors featuring rare and expensive stones and marbles, the church is also worth visiting for its beautiful wall frescoes, the best of which can be seen close to the entrance.

The tomb said to be that of St Nicholas in the southern aisle is actually of a later date, but there is another of the correct date that is now on display in the Archaeological Museum in Antalya (see page 68).

HOW PIOUS ST NICHOLAS BECAME JOLLY SANTA CLAUS

Christianity expanded quickly through the region after the 3rd century AD, and in the 4th century Myra became a bishopric. The first man to get the job was a local man, Nicholas, and he was said to have performed a number of miracles during his lifetime, including bringing several children back from the dead. He was made into a saint after his death.

The miracles St Nicholas performed made him the only sensible candidate for Patron Saint of Children and the 6th December was chosen as his saint's day. Over the centuries, in northern Europe and later in the United States, this religious St Nicholas gradually evolved into the jovial figure we know today, who wears his beard and robes because of the snowy December weather of the north.

Xanthos

One of the most illustrious cities in the ancient world – it was even mentioned in Homer's *Iliad* – Xanthos has a wonderful setting on a rocky outcrop with grand views down the whole of the wide fertile Xanthos river valley. The city was capital of Lycia for many centuries and one of its largest and most splendid settlements.

HISTORY

The roots of the city's history are wrapped in the myth surrounding King Iobates, who sent Bellerophon to kill the fire-breathing Chimaera and later shared his kingdom with him. The annals show the first mention of Xanthos in the Persian conquest of the surrounding valley in 540 BC. When they laid siege to the city, all the Xanthian men died defending their city while the women and children committed mass suicide. A second holocaust occurred under Roman rule in 42 BC when General Brutus attacked the city during the Roman civil war. Despite these events, the city prospered well into the Byzantine era and was an important centre for early Christianity.

In the 1840s, British explorer Charles Fellows rediscovered the site and, as was normal for the time, got permission from the Ottoman authorities to cart away the best pieces for the British Museum, including the pride of the collection, the Nereid Monument – an ornate 4th-century BC Ionic temple.

Today the remains are on the UNESCO list of World Heritage sites.
63 km (40 miles) east of Fethiye, west off the 400 Open 08.00–19.00 (May–Oct), 08.00–17.30 (Nov–Apr) Admission charge

HIGHLIGHTS

City gateway ★

This Hellenistic portal is inscribed with the names of the city's patrons, the gods and goddesses Apollo, Artemis and Leto. Close by is a better-preserved monumental arch dedicated to the Emperor Vespasian who ruled the Roman Empire 69–79 AD.

The Harpy Tomb ★

The tomb (the one here is a copy – Fellows took the original) is decorated with pairs of bird-women, assumed to be harpies. In Greek mythology these mythological winged creatures were young and beautiful, but later

Ancient remains at Xanthos are a UNESCO World Heritage Site

they were represented as hags with talons who carried sinful people off to the Underworld. Here they are seen carrying off children.

The Lycian Acropolis ★

There's not much left of the fortified centre of the city. Archaeologists think it was used right through from the Lycian era until well into the first century AD, so it would have undergone several rebuilding programmes. Look for segments of beautiful Roman and Byzantine mosaics underneath the protective layer of sand.

The Lycian Sarcophagus ★

When this pillar tomb dating from the 3rd century BC was opened, traces of human remains were discovered. It is thought that the sarcophagus was reused during the early Byzantine period because a later relief depicting funeral rituals was discovered with the bones.

The Roman Acropolis ★

On the hill behind the ticket office there are some interesting remains, through nothing worth mentioning individually. The remains of a large Byzantine basilica are undergoing excavations, but amongst the long grasses and woodland you can explore an early Byzantine monastery and there are lots of older Roman sarcophagi and Lycian rock tombs dotted around within the protection of some long sections of city wall.

The Roman theatre ★

Small but perfectly formed, the theatre's *cavea* or seating area is well preserved.

The Xanthian Obelisk ★

The remains of another tomb pillar that is inscribed with Lycian script and some Greek text that allowed scholars to translate the Lycian alphabet by comparing the two (apparently it tells of a Lycian man and his deeds of bravery that endowed his family with great prestige).

Patara

Ancient Patara used to be a wealthy city and the major port of Lycia until it silted up. It now symbolizes one of Turkey's dilemmas: how to make the most of tourist potential while preserving green credentials.

78 kms (48 miles) east of Fethiye, south off the 400
Open 07.30–19.00 (May–Oct); 08.30–17.00 (Nov–Apr)
One admission charge for site and beach

THINGS TO SEE & DO

The ancient site ★★

Patara nestles amongst wild grasses and sand dunes behind Patara beach. It was important in antiquity for its temple to Apollo, and was also a large naval base. Despite recent excavations, the sand has reclaimed a lot of the city. This is truly a place where you can pretend to be Indiana Jones, discovering the wonderful 1st-century AD city gate, a marvellous theatre and vast 2nd-century AD granaries.

The beach ★★

The longest beach in Turkey, Patara is also one of the most unspoilt because it is a protected turtle-nesting site. There is one lone beach bar and a single line of parasols at the eastern end of the 18 km (11 mile) stretch. The turtles nest at night, so it is off limits after dark from May to October, but during the day you can find a stretch of sand to yourself.

Gelemiş ★

The village of Gelemiş lies around 3 km (2 miles) inland from the beach, just north of the archaeological remains. At one time the site was due to be yet another tourist resort, but protection of the turtles stopped all that. Today, it is a low-key place with a handful of *gözleme* stalls, plus a couple of restaurant/bars and souvenir kiosks. The government still has not decided what it wants to do about development and, from time to time, the police close down unlicensed premises or issue eviction notices.

Ephesus

The largest and most complete ancient city in the eastern Mediterranean, Ephesus is a must-see site. The exceptionally well-preserved buildings, with little touches that bring the citizens to life, allow us to step back in time to the late Roman era, when this was the capital of Asia Minor. It is a long day trip from the Lycian region, but well worth the effort.

HISTORY

Founded in the 11th century BC, Ephesus became an important and rich city because it was the centre of worship for the goddess of fertility, Artemis. The temple here was one of the Seven Wonders of the Ancient World and attracted pilgrims from around ancient Greece.

In Roman times, the city was capital of the province with a population of over 250,000 people. It was a trading and banking city of immense wealth and was one of the most advanced cities in the Empire, with both flushing communal latrines and street lighting.

It was an important Christian city with a close association with St Paul of Tarsus and was populated until the 11th century AD. The last few hundred years brought serious problems when its port on the River Cayster began to silt up. Eventually it was cut off from the sea completely, making trade impossible. The city was then abandoned.

HIGHLIGHTS

The Upper City ★

A plateau at the top of the hill is the least exciting part of the city. Around the wide space that was once the Upper Agora, you will be able to explore the administrative headquarters, a small *odeon* (theatre) and the remains of a thermal spa. The best part of the upper city is the view down over the rest of Ephesus. From the small square in front of the Monument of Memmius, which was erected in homage to the citizens of the city, you get your most breathtaking view down Curetes Street, one of the most photographed vistas in Turkey.

Beyond the buildings, look out over the flat area where there is a modern airfield. This used to be port for the ancient city. Take some time to search for the coast in the distance. This is how far the sea has receded since Roman times and shows why the city was doomed. With no way to transport goods overland, the city couldn't function.

Ancient city of Ephesus

Curetes Street ★★★

The major arterial route linking the upper city with the port, Curetes Street had shops selling goods from around the empire, along with a number of important temples in between, including the Temple of Hadrian (built *c.* AD 117–138), with its distinctive double archway of fine Corinthian columns and elaborate frieze dedicated to the goddess Tyche.

Slope House ★★★

On each side of Curetes Street lie the residential quarters of Ephesus on the terraced hillside, reached by narrow alleyways. These were the houses of the rich, and one three-storey residence, Yamac Evleri (or Slope House) has undergone a thorough excavation to offer a glimpse of the Roman lifestyle and interior design. The spacious rooms are decorated with incredible original mosaic floors and wall frescoes that were the height of fashion. ❗ Extra admission charge, but it is worth it

Celcus Library ★★★

At the bottom of Curetes Street, the library is one of the focal points of the city. Erected in AD 117 as a memorial to Tiberius Julius Celsus by his son, it has a grandiose two-storey facade decorated with fluted columns and statues depicting The Four Virtues: Goodness (Arete), Thought (Ennoia), Knowledge (Episteme) and Wisdom (Sophia). The library once held 12,000 scrolls and was considered a great centre of learning.

Gate of Mazeus and Mithridates ★★

Linking the library and the neighbouring *agora*, the Gate of Mazeus and Mithridates was commissioned by two slaves freed by the Emperor Augustus who went on to become leading citizens of the city. It is built in the style of a triumphal arch.

Baths of Scolastica ★

The baths were one of the social centres of the city, a place where men got together to do business deals, debate politics or simply gossip. These were built in the 1st century AD in the heart of the city almost opposite the Celcus Library, and you can still see the hot room and cold room.

Theatre ★★★

One of the prettiest and most complete Roman theatres, Ephesus theatre is still used during the important Ephesus Festival of Culture and Art each May. During Roman times, 24,000 people would cram the stands to enjoy drama and comedy, but it was also the scene of many of St Paul's Evangelical speeches. He was cornered here by angry Ephesians when he criticised their beloved Artemis, but managed to escape.

Arcadian Way ★

One of the first Roman streets to get municipal lighting (in the 5th century AD), Arcadian Way led from the theatre to the port. The widest avenue in the city, much is now off limits, but it is possible to stand at the top (in front of the theatre) and look towards what would have been the warehouse district and the waterfront during Roman times.

Marble Way ★

Linking Curetes Street with Arcadian Way, the short Marble Way has a couple of interesting things to see. Notice how the marble of the road surface has been worn away by the passing of hundreds of thousands of cart wheels. No doubt these carts were heavily laden with goods for market. There is also an advertisement for a brothel etched in a stone of the road, pointing the way to the entrance close by.

Temple of Artemis ★

A kilometre away from the city is the Temple of Artemis or Artemision, the most important temple to Artemis in the ancient world. A mammoth building, it houses a life-size gold statue to the goddess. It was so impressive that it was known as one of the Seven Wonders of the Ancient World, but today it is a shadow of its former self. The Goths destroyed the site in AD 262 and much of the stone was later recycled – only the main temple platform and a couple of lonely columns remain.

Although the statue has never been found, there are several stone and marble statues of her in the Ephesus Museum at Selçuk (see below).

Ephesus Museum ★★★

If you visit the site of Ephesus, you must also visit the Ephesus Museum in the nearby town of Selçuk (Selchuk). This is where the best of the artefacts found at the site are on display.

The museum is not too big and overwhelming and includes the re-creation of a Roman room excavated at the site, complete with furniture and a small domestic shrine. The range of everyday objects on display is impressive, from hair pins to leather sandals. More precious objects include gold filigree jewellery and fine Samian tableware.

Several rooms display monumental statuary and friezes that decorated temples and public buildings, as well as the Hall of the Emperors, where statues and busts of many Roman leaders have been brought together. ⓐ 129 km (80 miles) north of Marmaris. Agora Çarşısı, Selçuk ◷ Open 08.30–noon and 13.30–17.30 ❶ Admission charge

Pamukkale

Pamukkale (Pamuk-alay) means 'cotton castle' in Turkish, and it is a most appropriate name. This huge natural travertine (a type of crystalline rock) fountain is one of the country's most famous attractions and one of its most beautiful and spectacular landscapes. Terraces of shallow limestone pools, the shape of oyster shells, cling to the hillside like a giant-stepped pool against the blue sky. From a distance it looks like piles of raw cotton, a crop that you find in fields all across this part of the country. Close up, the limestone is brilliant white and its edges glitter like diamonds – so bring your sunglasses!

THINGS TO SEE & DO

The Travertine Cascades ★★★

Several storeys of pure white shallow bowls are filled with azure blue waters shimmering in the sunshine. ⓐ 240 km (150 miles) north-east of Marmaris ⏲ 24 hours (ticket office manned during daylight hours) ❶ Admission fee charged when ticket office manned

Hierapolis ★★

The Romans loved natural springs, which they thought could cure various ailments. Hierapolis, the city they built here on top of the plateau next to Pamukkale, was really a giant spa town. Walk down the Cardo, the colonnaded main street to the Gate of Dominitian or explore the

HOW IT HAPPENS

The springs that emerge from the top of the hill in Pamukkale are rich in minerals. As the water cascades down the side of the hill, it leaves a microscopic layer of these minerals in any undulation on the ground and in the bowls of the pools. This turns white as it hardens. Over millions of years, these thin layers have built up and in some places at Pamukkale they are metres thick.

The Travertine Cascades at Pamukkale

necropolis (cemetery), with its collection of more than 1200 tombs and giant sarcophagi. The **museum** on site displays a range of items found during excavation of the site. ❶ Extra ticket charge

Pamukkale thermal baths ★★★

These baths have been open since Roman times and the modern buildings have been built directly on top of the ancient ones. While you are bathing, you can sit on fallen Roman columns that lie just under the surface of the water. The warm springs are said to be good for arthritis, stress and a long list of other ailments – although most people just come for the fun of swimming there. Even if you do not want to get wet (extra charge), come and have a look at the pools. ◷ Open 09.00–20.00

SAVING PAMUKKALE

In the early days, there was no protection for Pamukkale's delicate environment. People broke the sides of the pools as they climbed over them and sun oils from swimmers left a residue in the water that discoloured the white limestone. To add to this, several hotels that were built above the cascade began to use water from the spring for their own swimming pools, so it wasn't reaching the limestone pools to repair the damage. By the early 1990s 'cotton castle' was in real danger.

In the mid 1990s, the Turkish authorities instigated an action plan to save the Cascades. The hotels on the plateau have been bulldozed and the waters are being trained over the most damaged sections to make them white once again, a bit like teeth whitening. People have been banned from bathing in or walking on the pools. There is a footpath you can follow as long as you take your shoes off, but it is a bit painful for soft feet! All these changes have made a tremendous difference, the total area of white limestone has begun to expand again.

Food & drink

Turkish cuisine is considered to be one of the greatest in the world. Just like French or Chinese cuisine, it has had a huge influence on both what we eat and how we eat it. Though the days of the great Ottoman banquets are long gone, Turks still make meal times an event.

Freshness is the key to Turkish food – just look at the mountains of seasonal fruit and vegetables on sale in local markets or the seafood on ice at harbour-front restaurants for evidence of this. Dishes are generally cooked in olive oil, and a range of herbs and spices have traditionally been used to add flavour, but these are never overpoweringly strong.

WHEN TO EAT

Turks take a very relaxed approach to meal times. There will always be somewhere open no matter what time you get hungry, though you will find more of a social atmosphere between noon and 14.30 for lunch and between 19.00 and 22.00 for dinner, when other people head out to eat. Only the most formal restaurants close between lunch and dinner, and eateries of all kinds tend to stay open until the last client leaves.

In Turkey, food tends to be served warm rather than hot, which usually means chips arrive soggy not crisp. If you want yours piping hot, tell the waiter when you order.

WHERE TO EAT

Choosing these different styles of eateries depends on your appetite:

Kahve A Turkish coffee house that does not serve food and is usually a place for men to get together for a game of backgammon or a gossip.

Lokanta A casual, often family-owned restaurant serving a small range of home-cooked dishes. There probably will not be a printed menu, but it is normal to go into the kitchen to see what is being cooked. Point at what you want if the staff do not speak English.

Restoran A more formal restaurant than a *lokanta*. A *restoran* will have a printed menu with prices.
Kebapçi Specializes in grilled meats. They vary from pretty, family-owned establishments with outdoor terraces to small, urban kiosks.
Meyhane A bar- or pub-style place serving *meze* with drinks. Traditionally these have been for males only, but in tourist areas women will also be welcomed.
Pideçi These small snack bars serve Turkish pizza.
Bufes A basic snack bar.
Pastane Turkish patisseries serving cakes and pastries.

WHAT TO EAT

Meze dishes or starters

Turks prefer to eat *meze* style. That is where several small dishes are served at once and shared by everyone around the table. Try eating *meze* style for a truly authentic experience or order these dishes as a starter.

Cold options include *yaprak dolması* (stuffed vine leaves), fresh olives, *imam bayildi* (slices of aubergine with tomatoes and onions in olive oil) and *cacık* (a refreshing dip of natural yoghurt and cucumber with a hint of mint). Warm *meze* dishes include *borek* (filo pastry squares filled with cheese and herbs) and *midye dolması* (stuffed mussels).

Because Turks eat *meze* style (see above), you may find that if you order starters and main courses they will both arrive together. To avoid this, order only one course at a time.

Main courses

The most popular form of main course is grilled or barbecued meat, usually lamb, but you will also find some beef. It is grilled as chops or steak but also cubed and skewered for *şiş kebabs*, thinly sliced for *döner kebabs* or minced for *köfte* (meat balls) or *ıskender kebab* (minced meat wrapped around a skewer). Meat is always fresh and is generally served cooked through, not pink in the middle or rare.

Fresh fish is plentiful and delicious. You will find it elaborately displayed on ice at restaurant entrances. It is, however, always the most expensive item on the menu. It is sold by weight, so you choose a fish and it will be weighed and priced for you, then cooked to your specifications. If you find the price beyond your budget, you get the chance to change your mind before it is too late.

You will normally find that your main meal comes with bread and salad and either rice or chips.

Snacks

Turkey has excellent pizza (*pide* or *lahmacun*), though it is lighter than the Italian variety and often served rolled up so you can eat it on the go. Equally delicious are *döner kebabs*, slivers of lamb wrapped with salad in pitta bread, and you can find these on almost every street corner. *Gözleme* are pancakes or crepes with sweet or savoury fillings, while *semit* (bread rings sprinkled with sesame seeds) are perfect for stopping those afternoon hunger pangs.

Sweets

Turkish sweets and puddings are world renowned and make no apology for the amount of calories they contain. The most famous, *baklava* – layers of filo pastry soaked in butter, sprinkled with nuts then baked in honey syrup – is a work of art. Milk puddings are also popular, and are often delicious rich rice puddings evoking those you may have enjoyed as a child. *Lokum* or Turkish delight (a jelly sweet traditionally flavoured with rose water, but you will find many fruit flavours today) makes a great accompaniment to Turkish coffee.

If all this really sounds a little over the top, most *lokanta* and *restoran* offer fresh melon or other seasonal fruit as a lighter but equally delicious end to your meal. The sweet toothed will need to head to a specialist café for dessert. These are often very basic establishments with vinyl-topped tables and fluorescent lights, so they do not get points for romantic ambience, but they are full of authentic atmosphere.

TIPPING

Most *restoran* will add 10–15 per cent to your bill, but you should still leave a little something for the waiter. *Lokantas* will normally not add service to the bill but it is customary to leave 10–15 per cent. Leave small change on the table at bars and coffee houses.

International food

More and more 'international' food has become available in Turkey. This includes all-day English breakfasts if that is what you want, as well as other familiar items like pizzas and burgers. If you want to splash out, the large, upmarket hotels will have formal and expensive restaurants serving 'continental' menus with silver service.

Drinks

The usual array of fizzy soft drinks and international spirits are readily available, so you will certainly find something familiar during your trip. But why not try a particularly Turkish beverage? *Khave*, or Turkish coffee, is strong but never harsh and served in small cups. Take it *sade* (no sugar), *az şekerli* (a little sugar) or *çok şekerli* (sweet), but never try to empty the cup because there are grounds in the bottom. *Çay* (tea) is served weak without milk in tulip-shaped glasses. Apple tea is a refreshing alternative. Another delicious non-alcoholic drink is *ayran*, a refreshing natural-yoghurt drink. Bottled water is also readily available (don't drink water from the tap).

Turkey produces some excellent wine. Look for the trade names Doluca and Kavaklıdere for quality and reliability. It also brews a good, clean-tasting Pilsen-type beer under the brand name Efes, but for something more potent try *raki*, an anis-based spirit that is diluted with water. It is taken as both a before- or after-dinner drink, but at a strength of 40 per cent, should always be taken in moderation.

Menu decoder

A FEW BASIC WORDS

alabalık Freshwater trout
aşure Sweet 'soup' of fruits, nuts, pulses and bulgar wheat
balık Fish
barbunya Red mullet
beyti Minced kebab in pitta bread
bonfile Steak
borek Savoury pastry usually with cheese filling but can be meat
bülbül yuvası (swallow's nest) Shredded wheat in sugar syrup
çay Tea
çöp kebap Finely chopped meat or offal
dolma Vine leaves stuffed with rice and herbs
döner kebap Thin slices of grilled lamb sliced from a cone of meat
ekmek Bread
fasulye Haricot beans in tomato sauce
fırında sütlaç Oven-baked rice pudding usually served cold
gözleme A wafer-thin crepe with sweet or savoury filling
güllaç Flaky pastry and milk flavoured with nuts and rose water
güveç Meat and/or vegetable stew, cooked in a clay pot.
hamsi Anchovies
haydarı Yoghurt dip flavoured with garlic
imam bayıldı Translated as 'the imam fainted' – a classic Ottoman dish of baked aubergine with tomatoes and onions served cold
istakoz Lobster
ıskander kebab Minced meat cooked around a skewer and served in yoghurt or tomato sauce
kabak tatlısı Baked squash topped with clotted cream (*kaymak*)
kalamar Squid
karides Shrimp
karışık ızgara Mixed grill of lamb meat
karnıyarık Aubergines stuffed with minced lamb, currants and pine nuts then baked

karpuz Watermelon
kayısı Apricot
khave Turkish coffee
kiraz Cherry
kuzu Lamb
lahmacun A wafer-thin pizza topped with tomato sauce and minced lamb
levrek Sea bass
maden su Mineral water
manti Noodle dough ravioli parcels filled with meat
menemen Stir-fried omelette with hot peppers and vegetables
mercimak çorbası Lentil soup
midye Mussel
pastırma Dry-cured beef served thinly sliced
pide Small, flat pizzas with a thin topping of minced lamb or cheese
piliç Roast chicken
pirzola Lamb chops
pilav Rice
piyaz Haricot beans in vinaigrette
portakal Orange
salata Salad
şarap Wine
sardalya Sardine
sıgır Beef
siş kebab Cubes of meat put on a skewer then grilled
su Water
süt Milk
tarama Pink fish-roe paste
tavuk Boiled chicken
tel kadayıf Shredded wheat base smothered in honey syrup and chopped nuts
turşu Pickled vegetables
tuz Salt
yayla çorbası Rice soup
yoğurt çorbası Yoghurt soup

Shopping

There is something for everyone in Lycian Turkey, with a whole range of excellent souvenirs in all price brackets. You will be bombarded with designer rip-offs offering those must-have names at a fraction of the price back home. Stock up on items by your favourite fashion house, but check merchandise carefully, as quality varies from good to terrible.

Leather is also one of the top-ten buys for tourists. You will find a fantastic range of bags, belts and jackets. Again, designer names predominate but you can find traditional styles or have something made just for you.

Turkey is famous for its handicrafts and these include inlaid wooden items like small tables or chess sets, copper pots, rustic ceramics and pottery, onyx or Meerschaum pipes carved from a hard white clay found only in Turkey.

Gold and silver jewellery is also good value as items such as chains and bracelets are priced by weight. You can have things made at small jewellery workshops within a few days. Gold is usually 14-carat quality. Always check for the hallmark on gold and silver items.

The prize souvenir has to be the handmade Turkish carpet. These have been woven for centuries – each region has traditional patterns and colours. The best are made of silk, but most are wool.

Kilims are different to carpets because they have a flat weave rather than a pile. These are just as colourful but generally cheaper and they make great rugs and throws.

BROWSING

Browsing and window-shopping are not things the Turks do. When a shopkeeper sees you looking at his wares, he assumes you have an interest in buying. Obviously, they would rather you buy from them than from the shop next door, so they will put a lot of effort into getting you to stop, look and try.

BARTERING

World-famous Turkish carpets

Bartering or bargaining is a fact of life in Turkey. It is not something that comes naturally to a shopper who is used to fixed prices, but that doesn't mean it is something to be nervous or worried about. If you are in the market to buy an expensive souvenir such as a leather jacket or a Turkish carpet, you will be paying well over the odds if you simply pay what the shopkeeper asks.

There are several tips to make the bartering process more successful and enjoyable.

To start with, act cool about the specific item you want. Look at several items and then perhaps tell the shopkeeper you want to look in other shops to compare goods.

You will be offered a drink – Turkish tea or a soft drink – and it shows that you are more serious about buying if you accept.

Your first offer should be around 50 per cent of what the shop owner asks, then increase your offer little by little. You will probably end up paying around 70 per cent of the original asking price, but early or late in the season it could be more.

If you don't want to pay the price, simply tell the shop owner and walk away. He may call you back with a lower offer. Once you agree a price it is very bad manners to change your mind!

You will get a better price if you pay in cash rather than with a credit card, and better still if you pay in pounds sterling or euros rather than in Turkish Lira.

Kids

Turkey is an ideal destination for children. The simple pleasures of guaranteed sunshine, excellent beaches and warm water to play in will keep them happy for hours. Add to this the child-friendly environment, where children are welcomed in restaurants and cafés, and it makes for a very relaxed holiday. Exuberance is not frowned upon here. Turks love children and allow them the freedom to enjoy their childhood.

That said, you will find fewer attractions specifically aimed at children than in many European destinations. There are no children's museums, few 'theme' parks and no games arcades. But the jet skiing and water rides make up for that, as well as the chance to spot a wild dolphin or turtle during a boat trip.

TIPS FOR A CHILD-FRIENDLY TRIP

Turkish excursions can be heavy on history, and even the most enthusiastic adults can tire of this. Pace the sightseeing so you can alternate days of gazing at ancient buildings and tramping ancient streets with days by the pool or on the beach.

An afternoon siesta will help young children stay up late with the Turkish kids (who are often still playing in town squares until midnight). Early afternoon is also a good time to hide from the sun (see below).

CHOOSING RESORTS

You will need to think carefully about your Lycian resort if you have beach-loving children. The eastern section has few sandy bays and these tend to be on the small side. Often one enters the water from cement lidos or directly from the rocks, which doesn't suit young non-swimmers. The good news is that the beaches in the west are some of the best in Turkey, with safe long strands at **Ölüdeniz** (see page 24), **İztuzu** (see page 71) and **Patara** (see page 83). The last two are also turtle-nesting beaches where you may be lucky enough to spot one of these shy creatures just off shore.

Children are enthusiastically welcomed in Turkey

The **Dalyan boat trip** (see page 70) has something for everyone, and kids love to get covered in the sticky mud towards the end of the afternoon. The **Kekova boat trip** (see page 72) also offers the chance to swim and snorkel in crystal-clear water while gazing at a sunken Roman town.

TAKE CARE IN THE SUN

The Turkish sun is very hot and can damage young skin easily. Always ensure children wear a high-factor sun cream. Reapply this regularly, especially after they have been in the water.

Limit the time children spend in the sun, especially from noon through the early afternoon when it is at its strongest. Make sure they wear a hat and always carry a lightweight but long-sleeved garment for them in case shoulders and arms need covering up.

Keep children well hydrated – they may not complain of feeling thirsty but will need lots of liquid to keep them well.

Sports & activities

WALKING & HIKING

The Lycian coast is home to Turkey's most famous footpath, the 509 km (316 mile) Lycian Way, which begins at Fethiye and mirrors the coastline until it reaches Antalya on the Mediterranean coast. Of course, you don't need to attempt the whole walk to sample some of its delights. The easier sections lie in the west, but the best are the mountain sections in the east offering dramatic views down to the sea. The Turkish Tourist Board has produced a booklet about the route, available from tourist offices along the coast. Ⓦ www.thelycianway.com

If you fancy something more modest in scale, there is a wonderful short walk from **Ölüdeniz** over the hills to **Kayaköy** (see pages 22 and 28).

Boat trips are popular

WATER SPORTS

If you want water sports, choose one of the resorts in the west of the region (**Ölüdeniz**, **Marmaris** or **Çalış**) rather than in the east (**Kalkan** or **Kaş**) as the west has the best beaches. From jet skiing to banana boat rides, there is something for all the family.

SCUBA DIVING

The warm, clear waters around the Turkish coast make for great diving, but because of the wealth of ancient remains lying in the coastal shallows, many locations remain off limits and divers must be accompanied by a registered Turkish guide or dive master. If you are already qualified, bring your certification with you in order to book a guide.

If you want to learn to dive, most large resorts have schools accredited by the Professional Association of Diving Instructors (PADI), where you can be assured of good quality training. Many schools also offer taster sessions for people who have never dived before. After a little instruction, you will be allowed to do a dive under strict supervision – this is a great introduction to the sport.

YACHTING

Getting out onto the water is a wonderful way to tour Lycian Turkey, and a boat-based rather than hotel-based package holiday is a popular and easy option. British holiday companies offer several different routes for one- or two-week stays. See **Sunsail** (W www.sunsail.co.uk) or **Moorings** (W www.moorings.co.uk) for more details.

BOAT TRIPS

A huge flotilla of boats, including *gülets* (traditional wooden boats), offer day trips and these are good value for money, with lunch and drinks included. It could be to a remote beach or a historic site, but all offer delightful panoramic views of the Turkish coastline and a chance to spot a dolphin or turtle. The most popular are the **Dalyan boat trip** (see page 70) and the **Kekova boat trip** (see page 72). It pays to do a little research and price comparison. Check out what is included in the price before deciding. Tickets usually need to be booked the day before.

WINDSURFING

Most resorts on the western side of the Lycian coast have small schools offering lessons and board rentals. The gentler winds certainly suit the beginner and the improver. Kite surfing is a sport that is growing in popularity.

PARAGLIDING

Tandem jumps (with a qualified paraglider) from the peaks above **Kaş** and **Ölüdeniz** offer fantastic long-range views of the coast and a great adrenalin rush (see page 59)!

Festivals & events

Turkey's festivals and events reflect its fascinating and unique society. A secular republic, it is very proud of its fight for independence, marking the major events with great solemnity. However, over 90 per cent of its population are Muslim, so they also celebrate the main Islamic festivals, especially in the countryside. On top of this, Turkey holds a whole host of sporting competitions and folkloric festivals.

CIVIL CELEBRATIONS

23 April National Sovereignty and Children's Day celebrates the establishment of the first Grand National Assembly in 1920, which saw the end of the Ottoman Empire.

19 May Atatürk Day and Youth and Sports Day marks the beginning of the Turkish War of Independence in 1919, when Atatürk rallied the country to fight the forces who had divided Turkish territory after World War I.

30 August Victory Day celebrates the success of Turkish forces over the Greek army in 1922.

29 October Republic Day marks the date when the present Turkish Republic was declared in 1923.

10 November Atatürk's Death: although not a holiday, Turks mark the day of Atatürk's death in a very poignant way. At 09.05 on 10 November, the exact time of his death, the whole country comes to a standstill for a minute of silent remembrance.

MAJOR MUSLIM CELEBRATIONS

The Muslim calendar runs on a lunar cycle different from that of our solar Gregorian calendar. These celebrations change date each year.

Ramadan (Ramazan)

For the entire ninth month (30 days) of the Muslim year, Muslims fast between dawn and dusk. This marks the time when Mohammed wandered in the desert and Allah revealed the verses of the Koran to him. Muslims devote Ramazan to prayer, reflection and charity.

Şeker Bayramı (the Sugar Festival)

This three-day festival (pronounced she-ker bay-ramer) celebrates the end of Ramazan. Families party together enjoying traditional foods, particularly sugary foods such as baklava, pastries and lokum.

Kurban Bayramı

This is the festival that commemorates the prophet Abraham offering his son Isaac to Allah or God (when Allah accepted the sacrifice of a sheep instead). It takes place during the tenth month of the Muslim year.

Other Muslim festivals

Other major and minor festivals are not necessarily holidays but are the times for special prayers and family get-togethers, including:

Aflure Günü (*ah-shoo-reh gew-new*) The tenth day of the Islamic lunar month of Muharrem commemorates Adam repenting his sin, the birth of the Prophet Abraham, Jonah's deliverance from the whale and the martyrdom of Islamic hero Hüseyin. Also, Turks celebrate Noah's ark coming to rest on dry land.

Mevlid-i Nebi (*mehv-leed ee neh-bee*) The Prophet Mohammed's birthday is celebrated with mosque illuminations and special foods.

Three other days of celebration where mosques are decorated and lit up are: **Regaip Kandili**, the 'Beginning of the Three Moons'; **Berat Kandili**, the 'Day of Forgiveness'; and **Miraç Kandili**, celebrating the Prophet Mohammed's ascent into heaven.

Circumcision ceremonies

Circumcision is an important milestone in the life of a young Turkish boy and takes place at any time between birth and the age of seven. The child is dressed in new clothes – often a bright satin suit and a light blue headdress, and then paraded around the town visiting family and friends. This was traditionally on horseback but today could be in a parade of cars that travels the streets with horns blaring. After the ceremony there is a big family party.

OTHER MAJOR EVENTS IN THE LYCIAN REGION

April

- On 23 April, **Marmaris Children's Festival** is one of the best places to celebrate Children's Day.

May

- The **International Sailing Festival** in Marmaris sees craft from all around the Mediterranean.

June

- The **Abdal Musa Literary Festival** is held at Elmalı (inland from Kaş).
- The **International Lycian Festival** at Kaş (end June–early July) brings together folkloric performances from around Turkey.

July

- Early in the month the **International Festival of the Sea** at Marmaris, and the **Manavgat Tourism Festival**.

October

- Late in the month is an **international *gület* festival** at Bozburun, west of Marmaris.
- Late October or early November is the **international sailing regatta** in Marmaris

December

- A month of activities at Myra marks the feast of St Nicholas, culminating in the 24 December for the **Santa Claus Festival**.

PRACTICAL INFORMATION
Tips & advice

Preparing to go

GETTING THERE

Turkey is a popular destination and features in the brochures of all the major package tour operators with a range of hotels and holidays in all price brackets. Prices are highest when demand is high, such as during school holiday periods, when it is wise to book as early as possible, especially if you have children.

If you are more flexible, it will be less busy and cheaper to travel early (May/June) or late in the season (September/October), when last-minute bargains are possible. Teletext, the Internet or travel agents offer ways to compare prices and facilities whatever time of year you want to travel. If you want to organize your own package you can book a scheduled flight (flexible dates) or charter flight (fixed dates of one or two weeks' duration) and find your own accommodation. Many hotels have their own websites that allow you to make and confirm booking, or use specialist companies such as **Expedia** (Ⓦ www.expedia.co.uk), **Travelocity** (www.travelocity.co.uk) or **Priceline** (www.priceline.co.uk).

You should also check the travel supplements of the weekend newspapers such as the *Sunday Telegraph* and *Sunday Times*. They often carry adverts for inexpensive flights and privately owned villas and apartments to rent.

By air

Most visitors to the Lycian coast arrive via the airport at **Dalaman** in the west of the Lycian region. This caters to charter-holiday companies with flights from many UK airports during the holiday season (April–October).

There are no international scheduled flights into Dalaman. If travelling by scheduled flight, you will need to take a flight into Istanbul and then fly out from there with **Turkish Airlines**, the national airline. It operates several flights a day throughout the year.

The airport has duty-free shops, exchange bureaux, car-rental offices and taxis, but services are limited if you arrive or depart at night.

TOURIST INFORMATION

For more information about Turkey before you leave, contact the **Turkish Culture and Tourism Office** (@ 170–173 Piccadilly, London W1J 9EJ t 0207 629 7771 f 0207 491 0773 w www.gototurkey.co.uk).

BEFORE YOU LEAVE

Holidays are supposed to be relaxing, so take a little time and plan ahead. You do not need inoculations to travel to Turkey but it would be wise to make sure that your family is up to date with shots like tetanus. It is also worth having a dental check-up before you go.

It is sensible to carry a small first-aid kit with items such as painkillers, treatment for upset stomachs, travel/sea-sickness tablets, plasters, antiseptic ointment and insect repellent. Sun cream is more expensive in Turkey, so buy this before you go. If you take any prescription medication make sure you have enough for the duration of your holiday.

DOCUMENTS

The most important documents you will need are tickets and passports. Make sure that passports for all members of the family are up to date. Children already named on a parent's passport can travel without their own passports, but any recent additions to the family or children not on a passport already will need to have their own. These can take up to 28 days to be issued by the passport office, although you can pay more for a quicker service. If your passport has less than three months to run on the date you arrive in Turkey, you need to renew it before you go. For further information on how to renew you passport and for current processing times, get in touch with the **Passport Agency** (t 0870 521 0410 w www.ukpa.gov.uk). When your tickets arrive from the travel agent check that all the names, dates and times are correct.

Keep passports and travel tickets or confirmations in a safe place. If possible keep photocopies of your passport numbers and ticket information (and travellers' cheques if you take them) separately.

If you are going to hire a car while in Turkey all named drivers need to have their driver's licences with them.

MONEY

Always change a small amount of currency before you leave, especially if your flight arrives late in the evening or early in the morning. You can do this at a post office, travel agent (allow two or three days for the money to arrive) or at the airport just before you fly. Make sure that your credit and debit cards are up to date before you travel.

Changing money Banks can be found in all major towns. There are plenty of exchange bureaux in resorts. Before you change money check the exchange and commission rates. You will find cashpoints in the larger resorts, but not all smaller resorts.

Travellers' cheques Provide the safest way to carry money since they can be replaced if lost or stolen (remember to note down the cheque numbers in the event of needing to have them replaced). Order them from a bank or travel agent at least a week before you leave on holiday. Travellers' cheques can be cashed at banks, exchange bureaux and many hotels.

ATM machines These are widespread in the resort areas. You can obtain cash with either your Maestro Card or credit card provided you have a Personal Identification Number (PIN). Your bank or credit card company may charge more for this service.

Credit cards These are becoming more widely accepted in shops and restaurants but not in cheaper *lokantas* and *pide* stalls or in the markets, so do not rely on this as your only method of payment.

You can often pay in pounds rather than in Turkish Lira, so it pays to take some British cash; remember to keep this secure.

INSURANCE

Check that your insurance policy covers you adequately for loss of possessions and valuables, for activities you might want to try – such as horse-riding or water sports – and for emergency medical and dental treatment, including flights home, if required. Note also that UK visitors are not entitled to reduced-cost or free medical treatment, as Turkey is not, at the time of writing, a part of the EEA.

CLIMATE

The coastal areas of western Turkey have a Mediterranean climate. This means long, hot dry summers, mild winters with some rain and short, warm springs and autumns.

Average daytime temperatures are: April – 20°C (68°F); May – 24°C (75°F); June – 29°C (84°F); July – 31°C (88°F); August – 32°C (90°F); September – 29°C (84°F); October – 24°C (75°F).

In summer you will only need light clothing – breathable and natural fabrics are best – but take lightweight trousers and a long-sleeved shirt to cover your arms and legs in case you get sunburnt.

Early or late in the season take a warmer layer like a light fleece just in case it gets a bit chilly in the evenings.

PETS

Make sure your pets are cared for while you are away. A neighbour may come in to feed them, or book larger animals such as cats or dogs into a pet hotel. These can be full in summer, so make reservations early.

SECURITY

Take sensible precautions to prevent your house being burgled while you are away:

- Cancel milk, newspapers and other regular deliveries so that post and milk does not pile up on the doorstep, indicating that you are away.
- Let the postman know where to leave parcels and bulky mail (ideally with a next-door neighbour) that will not go through your letterbox.
- If possible, arrange for a friend or neighbour to visit regularly, closing and opening curtains in the evening and morning, and switching lights on and off to give the impression that the house is being lived in.
- Consider buying electrical-timing devices that will switch lights and radios on and off, again to give the impression that there is someone in the house.

- Let Neighbourhood Watch representatives know that you will be away so that they can keep an eye on your home.
- If you have a burglar alarm, make sure that it is serviced and working properly and is switched on when you leave (you may find that your insurance policy requires this). Ensure that a neighbour is able to gain access to the alarm to turn it off if it is set off accidentally.
- If you are leaving cars unattended, put them in a garage, if possible, and leave a key with a neighbour in case the alarm goes off.

SPECIAL MEALS

Do not forget that you need to book special in-flight meals (for example, vegetarian, vegan or diabetic) well in advance – preferably when the booking is made, but otherwise at least two weeks in advance of your departure.

AIRPORT PARKING & ACCOMMODATION

Book airport parking or overnight accommodation close to the airport as soon as you have booked your holiday. Demand for both is high, especially in the summer. Some hotels offer free parking for a one- or two-week holiday if you book rooms with them.

BAGGAGE ALLOWANCES

Baggage allowances are becoming more strict and the price of excess baggage (that over the amount allowed as part of your ticket) is expensive. Currently scheduled flights allow 20 kg (44 lb) of checked-in baggage (bags that go into the hold) per passenger, but charter flights have lower limits, as little as 15 kg (33 lb) for clients who have booked at the last minute or bought a flight-only package. Your tour company will tell you your limit and it will be printed on your ticket. Each passenger is also allowed to carry a small bag (5 kg/11 lb) onto the plane, plus duty-free shopping and items such as laptop computers or cameras.

If you think you may want to take more than this allowance, ask about buying extra baggage capacity before you travel (preferably at the same time as you book your ticket). Many airlines can sell extra capacity to you that will be much less expensive than would be the case if you just turned up at the check-in desk with overweight bags.

If you are going to be travelling with a large item – a push-chair, golf clubs or surf board, for example – let the holiday company know when you make the booking. There may be an extra charge for these.

CHECK-IN, PASSPORT CONTROL & CUSTOMS

For first-time travellers, airport procedures and security can be a little intimidating but the process is simple and straightforward.

Check-in desks usually open two or three hours before a flight is scheduled to leave. Leave the house so that you arrive early at the airport. This will give you a good choice of seat and help avoid any unforeseen delay en route that will make you miss your flight. Most airports have good restaurant and café facilities and it is better to wait in them for your flight time rather than to stress over being late. You can always use this time to read up on your holiday destination.

Look for your flight number on the TV monitors in the check-in area and find the relevant check-in desk. Your tickets will be checked and your luggage taken. Take your boarding card and go to the departure lounge through the security check area. Here your hand luggage will be x-rayed and your passport checked.

In the departure lounge, you can still shop for duty-free goods, but watch the monitors that tell you when to board – usually about 30 minutes before take-off. Go to the departure gate shown and follow the instructions given you by the airline staff.

Because Turkey is outside the EU you will be allowed to purchase goods 'duty free'. You will not be allowed to take more than the following amounts of duty-free goods into Turkey.

- 200 cigarettes or 50 cigars or 200g of tobacco
- 5 litres (9 pt) of alcohol

During your stay

AIRPORTS

There is good road access to the region's airports, but if you are returning a rental car at the end of your holiday allow plenty of time to reach the airport and check in for your flight. If your flight departs at night, the airport will have limited facilities during your wait, so it might be wise to take drinks and snacks. Also, duty-free shops may not be open at night.

CURRENCY

In January 2005, Turkey devalued its currency and issued new notes and coins. The Yeni (New) Turkish Lira or YTL replaced the old Turkish Lira, and each new Lira is worth 1,000,000 old Lira. Yeni Lira come in note denominations of 1, 5, 10, 20, 50 and 100 Lira. Each Yeni Lira is made up of 100 Kuruş, which come in coins of 1, 5, 10, 25 and 50 Kuruş. There is also a 1 Lira coin.

ELECTRICITY

Power is 220 volts, 50 cycles. Plugs are European style with two round pins so you will need an adapter for your electrical appliances.

EMBASSIES & CONSULATES

The British Embassy ⓐ Sehit Ersan Caddesi 46/A, Çankaya, Ankara ⓣ 0312 455 3344

Honorary Consul Marmaris c/o Yesil Marmaris Tourism and Yacht Management Inc ⓐ Barbaros Caddesi 118 (P O Box 8), Marina, 48700 Marmaris ⓣ 0252 412 6486, ext 36 and 39

> **TELEPHONING TURKEY**
>
> To call Turkey from the UK, dial 00 90 followed by the city code (without the initial 0), then the 7-digit number.

FACILITIES FOR VISITORS WITH DISABILITIES

Turkey is working hard to improve facilities for the disabled but provision is still patchy. Many newly built hotels and public buildings have facilities but access to archaeological sites and historic buildings is difficult and the lack of curb ramps and controlled street crossings in towns makes movement problematical. If necessary, contact the hotels direct to ensure that they can provide what you need. For further help, contact **Holiday Care International** – they have information about facilities and accessibility in destinations for travellers with disabilities (ⓐ 7th Floor, Sunley House, 4 Bedford Park, Croydon, Surrey CR0 2AP ⓣ 0845 124 9971 ⓦ www.holidaycare.org.uk).

GETTING AROUND

Car hire The easiest way to rent a car is to book it in the UK at the same time as you book your holiday. This way you can be clear about costs and correct insurance cover. It is also easy to rent a car in Turkey if you decide you want a couple of days or more on the road. At your resort, your representative will be able to help you, or visit a local car-rental office. Check the quality of the cars before you rent.

You will need to leave a deposit and show your driving licence. For all car rentals, make sure you get a contact telephone number in case you have mechanical problems. Drivers must be over 21 years of age (some companies 25 years) and have held a full licence for at least one year.

Driving In Turkey you drive on the right and overtake on the left (the opposite of the UK). Speed limits are 50 km/h (31 mph) in urban areas, 90 km/h (56 mph) on main roads and 120 km/h (75 mph) on motorways and dual carriageways – unless the signs indicate another limit. Seat belts are compulsory in front seats and back seats where fitted.

The main coast road and other major roads are generally in good condition, but small roads vary in quality and some are dirt surface rather than asphalt.

You will meet all kinds of traffic on the roads, from large, modern trucks to donkey and carts (and the occasional loose farm animal).

You will need to be on the alert for slower moving vehicles. Slower traffic will usually move onto the hard shoulder to allow you to pass.

If Turkish drivers want to cross the traffic, they will often pull over to the right and let traffic behind them pass before making the turn so they do not hold everyone up.

When traffic is quieter (at night and on Sundays), Turkish traffic lights are switched to flashing amber. This means that you will need to pay attention because there is a junction or crossroads ahead that is not controlled.

Parking is a problem in all the major resorts. Do not park where you see a yellow kerb.

You will find both leaded and unleaded petrol. Not all fuel stations are self-service. A member of staff may come and clean your windscreen. This is at no extra cost, but staff will appreciate a small tip. Some petrol stations do not accept credit cards.

Long distance bus services All Turkish towns and cities are served by an efficient, modern and cheap bus network that makes an excellent framework for touring the country. The services feature air conditioning, videos (in Turkish, of course), refreshments and programmed stops for meals.

Local buses The dolmuş is the lifeblood of local transport. These small mini-vans run set routes, leaving the terminus when full and picking up passengers anywhere along the route. There will usually be a service from town to the main beaches and resort hotels. They are cheap and efficient.

HEALTH MATTERS

Should you require medical help, most hotels will have a doctor on call but you will be charged for the consultation (you can usually claim this back from your holiday insurance policy).

Hospital If you need to stay in hospital there are clean, though limited, facilities in most large towns, smaller clinics in smaller towns. Staff are well trained and most doctors can speak some English. You have to pay for treatment but depending on circumstances this could be organized directly through your insurance company. If you have travelled on a package holiday with a major tour company, your resort representative will be able to offer advice and help.

Pharmacies (Ezcane) Pharmacists in Turkey are highly qualified and most will speak some English. They will be able to advise you on treatments for complaints such as minor sunburn, upset tummy, insect bites and diarrhoea. Normal opening hours are from 09.00 to 19.00 hours and there will be a duty pharmacist available in every town.

Water Although tap water is clean, only drink bottled or boiled water.

THE LANGUAGE

Turkish is a relatively new language. It was developed in the 1920s by Kemal Atatürk, the first President of the Turkish Republic, to replace Arabic.

Pronunciation

Turkish uses the Latin alphabet. Every letter in each Turkish word is pronounced, even when there is a double letter. For example, the word *saat* (hour), is pronounced 'sa-at'. All letters are pronounced as in English except the following:

c which is pronounced as a 'j' as in 'Jerry'
ç which is pronounced 'ch' as is 'chaffinch'
ğ which is a silent or soft g, it lengthens the sound of the letter before it
ı (a dotless ı) and is pronounced 'a' as in the first syllable of 'another'
ö as in the 'u' in fur
ş pronounced 'sh' as in 'ship'
ü pronounced as the French 'tu'

ENGLISH	TURKISH
Useful words & phrases	
Hello	*merhaba*
Good morning	*günaydin*

ENGLISH	TURKISH
Good evening	*iyi akşamlar*
Good night	*iyi geceler*
Goodbye (said by those departing)	*allahaısmarladık*
Goodbye (said by those remaining)	*güle güle*
Yes	*evet*
No	*yok* or *hayir*
Please	*lutfen*
Thank you	*mersi* or *teşekkur ederim*
Do you speak English?	*Ingilizce biliyormusunuz*
I don't understand	*anlamıyorum*
I understand	*anlıyorum*
I don't know	*bilmiyorum*
The bill	*hesap*

General Vocabulary

Bus	*autobüs*
Small local bus	*dolmüş*
Ferry	*feribot*
Port	*limani*
Plane	*uçak*
Airport	*hava limani*
Ladies (toilet)	*bayanlar*
Mens (toilet)	*baylar*
Left	*sağa*
Right	*sola*
Straight ahead	*doşdogru*
How much is this?	*ne kadar* or *ne kaça*
Money (cash)	*para*
Too expensive	*çok pahalı*
Travellers' cheques	*seyahat çeki*
Do you sell stamps?	*Posta pulu var mı?*
Open	*açik*

ENGLISH	TURKISH
Postage stamp	*pul*
Closed	*kapalı*
Credit card	kredi kartı
Today	*bugün*
Yesterday	*dün*
Tomorrow	*yarın*
Where is?	*nerede*
Mosque	*cami*
Market or bazaar	*çarşı*
Mountain	*daş*
Street	*sokak* (often abbreviated to *sok*)
Avenue	*caddesi* (often abbreviated to *cad*)
Place	*meydani* (often abbreviated to *meyd*)
Boulevard	*Bulvari* (abbreviated to *Bul*)
Call the police!	*polise haber verin!*
What time is it?	*saat kaç?*
Duty pharmacy	*nöbeçi ezcane*
Doctor	*doktor*
Emergency exit	*imdat Çikişi*
Hospital	*hastane*
Room	*oda*
Toilet	*tuvalet*
Shower	*duş*
Towel	*havlu*

Numbers

One	*bir*
Two	*iki*
Three	*üç*
Four	*dört*
Five	*beş*
Six	*altı*

ENGLISH	TURKISH
Seven	*yedi*
Eight	*sekiz*
Nine	*dokuz*
Ten	*on*
One hundred	*yüz*
One thousand	*bin*
Days of the week	
Monday	*pazartezi*
Tuesday	*salı*
Wednesday	*çarşamba*
Thursday	*perşembe*
Friday	*cuma*
Saturday	*cumartesi*
Sunday	*pazar*

LAUNDRY

There are few public laundry facilities in Turkey. Most large hotels offer laundry and dry-cleaning services at a price premium.

LOST PROPERTY

If it is possible, retrace your steps. Turks are honest people by nature and someone may have it in safekeeping for you.

- If you have a rep, report the matter to them and ask their advice.
- Visit the nearest police station to report your loss.
- Report any lost credit cards to the credit-card company immediately.
- Report any lost passport to your nearest embassy or consulate immediately.

MAKING A COMPLAINT

If you want to make a complaint about anything that happens during your holiday, explain as simply as you can what the problem is. Stay calm and do not lose your temper. Your holiday representative is there to help make your holiday as enjoyable as possible. See them for any complaint about your flight or hotel. In restaurants or shops, ask to speak to the manager or owner.

MEDIA

The only English-language newspaper printed in Turkey is the *Turkish Daily News*. The popular English tabloids are widely available in all the leading resorts at a price premium, though they may be a day old. Most upmarket hotels will offer *BBC News 24* as part of their programming. Resort bars will often transmit Premier League matches live, and show English news reports. You will find Internet cafés in most resorts.

OPENING HOURS

Opening hours for museums and archaeological sites change all the time. It is probably best not to arrive too early or too late at a site in case the ticket office is closed. For most places in Turkey, as with the rest of the Mediterranean, it is best to avoid arriving during the lunch hours, as most places will shut for a long lunch. Also be aware of seasonal variations – in the off-season, many places will shut entirely or have reduced hours.

Banks 08.30–noon and 13.30–17.00 (Mon–Fri)
Shops 09.00–19.00 (Mon–Sat); tourist shops daily 09.00–22.00 in the resorts in summer
Government offices 08.30–12.30 and 13.30–17.30 (Mon–Fri)
State museums 08.30–17.30 (Tues–Sun); closed for lunch in winter
Archaeological sites 08.00–18.00 or 19.00 in summer

POST OFFICES

Post offices have yellow signs with the black letters PTT on them. Most post offices are open government office hours and offer postal and telecommunications services. Most shops selling postcards will also sell stamps for a small price premium.

PUBLIC TOILETS

There are few public toilet facilities in Turkey. The best policy is to stop at a café or bar. These are not always of a high standard and some may be the 'hole in the floor' Continental-type toilets. If in a resort, visit the nearest hotel. These facilities should be modern and clean. Always carry a supply of toilet roll or tissue, as few toilets outside the hotels will have a supply. In museums and archaeological sites you may have to pay a small amount for use of the facilities. Keep small change handy for this.

RELIGION

Turkey is a predominantly Muslim country, though it is one of the most liberal Islamic populations in the world. Alcohol and gambling are allowed. The countryside is generally more conservative than the coastal resorts. If you are travelling away from the coast, or wanting to visit mosques or churches, modest dress would be appropriate and respectful.

SAFETY & SECURITY

Turkey is a safe country and you are very unlikely to find yourself the victim of a serious incident. However, petty crime such as theft can be guarded against with a few simple rules.

- Don't carry large amounts of cash or valuables with you. Take only what you need for the day.
- Leave nothing on show in your car.
- Don't leave valuables unguarded on the beach or at cafes.
- Keep to well-lit streets at night.
- If you are unsure of the route back to your hotel or apartment, take a taxi.
- Be sure to report any stolen credit cards to the credit-card company immediately.
- Report any stolen passport to your nearest embassy or consulate immediately.

TELEPHONING ABROAD

To call an overseas number from Turkey, dial 00 followed by the country code (UK=44) and the area code (minus the initial 0), then the rest of the number.

USEFUL TELEPHONE NUMBERS

- **Long distance operator** 131
- **International reverse charge calls** 115
- **International directory enquiries** 161

TELEPHONES

Most resorts have modern public phone boxes that will offer international direct dialling to the UK. These will operate with major credit cards or phone cards that can be purchased at press kiosks, tourist offices and post offices.

Your personal mobile phone should also work, though the cost of calls is a lot higher than local rates at home. Check this with your service provider before you leave.

Most upmarket and resort hotels will offer international direct dialling that will allow you to phone home from your room, but beware of these, as they often charge a high premium. Ask about rates before making the call.

TIME DIFFERENCES

Turkey is two hours ahead of Greenwich Mean Time (GMT) throughout the year.

TIPPING

In restaurants, it is advisable to leave 10–15 per cent of the bill, plus some small change for the waiting staff. In cafés and bars, leave a tip of small change. Bell-boys should receive one 50 Kuru (see

Currency, page 114) per bag, room cleaners in hotels should be left 50 Kuru per day, and shoe guardians in mosques welcome a small tip.

WEIGHTS & MEASURES

Turkey uses the metric system, so has grams and kilograms, millilitres and litres, metres and kilometres. Use the following conversion table to know the correct weights and measures.

Imperial to metric

1 inch = 2.54 centimetres
1 foot = 30 centimetres
1 mile = 1.6 kilometres
1 ounce = 28 grams
1 pound = 454 grams
1 pint = 0.6 litres
1 gallon = 4.6 litres

Metric to imperial

1 centimetre = 0.4 inches
1 metre = 3 feet, 3 inches
1 kilometre = 0.6 miles
1 gram = 0.04 ounces
1 kilogram = 2.2 pounds
1 litre = 1.8 pints

INDEX

ACKNOWLEDGEMENTS

We would like to thank all the photographers, picture libraries and organisations for the loan of the photographs reproduced in this book, to whom copyright in the photograph belongs:
JupiterImages Corporation (pages 101, 107, 125);
Patrick Anthonisz/Alamy (page 77);
Thomas Cook Tour Operations Ltd (pages 1, 5, 9, 11, 17, 20, 28, 30, 33, 35, 44, 48, 51, 53, 55, 57, 63, 67, 80, 85, 89, 91, 99, 102).

We would also like to thank the following for their contribution to this series:
John Woodcock (map and symbols artwork);
Becky Alexander, Patricia Baker, Sophie Bevan, Judith Chamberlain-Webber, Nicky Gyopari, Stephanie Horner, Krystyna Mayer, Robin Pridy (editorial support);
Christine Engert, Suzie Johanson, Richard Lloyd, Richard Peters, Alistair Plumb, Jane Prior, Barbara Theisen, Ginny Zeal, Barbara Zuñiga (design support).